Seen and Heard

Seen and Heard

A Century of Arab Women in Literature and Culture

BY MONA N. MIKHAIL

OLIVE
BRANCH
PRESS

An imprint of Interlink Publishing Group, Inc.
Northampton, Massachusetts

First published in 2004 by

OLIVE BRANCH PRESS
An imprint of Interlink Publishing Group, Inc.
46 Crosby Street, Northampton, Massachusetts 01060
www.interlinkbooks.com

Library of Congress Cataloging-in-Publication Data

Mikhail, Mona.
Seen and heard : a century of Arab women in literature and culture /
by Mona Mikhail.—First American ed.
p. cm.
ISBN 1-56656-463-8 (pbk.)
1. Arabic literature—20th century—History and criticism. 2. Women
in literature. 3. Women, Arab. I. Title.
PJ7538.M554 2003
892.7'09352042'0904—dc21
2003014171

Permission to reprint the following essays is gratefully acknowledged: Chapter 11
originally appeared in *Arabic Literature in North Africa: Critical Essays and Annotated
Bibliography* (Cambridge, MA: Dar Mahjar Publishing, 1982) and Chapter 8 in
ALIF: Journal of Poetics 19 (1999).
In a slightly different form, Chapters 13 and 14 appeared in the author's *Studies in the
Short Fiction of Mahfouz and Idris* (New York, NY: New York University Press, 1992).

Printed and bound in Canada by Webcom

To request our complete 40-page full-color catalog,
please call us toll free at **1-800-238-LINK,** visit our
website at **www.interlinkbooks.com,** or write to
Interlink Publishing
46 Crosby Street, Northampton, MA 01060
e-mail: info@interlinkbooks.com

CONTENTS

ACKNOWLEDGEMENTS

To write about a subject about which one has spent almost an academic lifetime of research is to acknowledge a profound indebtedness to many who have contributed to the growing field of women's studies both in this country and in the Arab world. More than two decades ago I wrote *Images of Arab Women: Fact and Fiction* (1979), then considered one of the earliest works in the field. Today the floodgates have opened in almost every discipline—history, anthropology, literature, law, among others—uncovering new research that has forever altered our traditional perceptions.

I therefore would like to recognize the insights of colleagues, students, and friends too many to mention here, who continue to provide me with encouragement, support, and friendship. I am also indebted to Pam Thompson, my editor, for her patience, encouragement, and standards of excellence.

The choice of what to include in such a work is ultimately personal, and some would say political. The story of women in the Arab world at this critical juncture in history defies traditional classifications, and hence the decisions of what to include from a century of writing about women and by women was, to say the least, a challenging task.

Women's issues in the Arab world are not limited to access to education, equal opportunity, or reproductive freedoms. The experience of Arab women rather as agents in history, producers of literature, contributors to culture, whose voices attempt at breaking a "deafening silence" has been the impetus for this work.

In the wake of wars and conflicts that have spilled into the 21st century, Arab women are busy mourning, trying to save the wounded, and fighting waves of religious fanaticism that threaten to dislodge their hard won gains in the 20th century. My hope is that these studies capture the discourses of both male and female feminist writings and bring to the fore possibilities of transformation that could alter the threats of cultural forms of oppression that lurk in the wake of these repeated conflicts and wars.

I dedicate this work to the memory of my mother whose resilience, sense of humor, and affection have inspired me all along. I hope that all the men and women in my family, especially the second generation born in this country—my mother's grandchildren and great-grandchildren—will grow up to appreciate the challenges of their shared heritage.

If women have in the past been silenced and all too often denied visibility, then the hope that these studies will valorize their brave attempts to be seen and heard.

We are told that all literature seeks to leave traces of its emergence in space and time and proceeds to invent worlds in order to assure its own existence. Certainly Arabic literature directs its imaginary projection to questioning and searching for answers to its bewildering realities. Indeed, the uncertainties and crises of the contemporary Arab world are amply manifest in its diverse literary and cultural manifestations.

The relationship between a writer and her/his language and the underlying urgency of writing are revealed in the wide variety of their writings and artistic expressions. The spaces and the worlds of fiction recreated in the imaginations of Arab writers (male and female) are analyzed here both stylistically and thematically, in studies that span the work of several of the 20th century's generations. Some are the pioneering reformists and champions of women's causes, such as the great Rifaa al Tahtawi, who wrote in the middle of the 19th century, clamoring for equal education and rights for girls (see Chapter 12). Or the prince of poets, Ahmad Shawqi, whose poetic dramas heralded new roles for women (see Chapter 8). Or Nabawiyya Musa, a remarkable activist and reformist writing in the early 20th century, whose bold castigations of a bigoted hierarchy is contrasted here to the retrograde positions of late 20th-century thinkers (see Chapter 7).

The fiction of major contemporary writers from both the Arab east and North Africa, such as Tawfiq al-Hakim, Naguib Mahfouz, Yusuf Idris, Assia Djebar, and Rachid Boudjedra, is deconstructed to enable us to re-create their worlds. Of course, we cannot reduce these works to purely intellectual definitions. As readers we can merely visit these spaces and worlds of fiction and attempt to assess momentary aspects of their experiences (see Chapters

10–14), before returning to our own shared world.

As we enter a new millennium, women throughout the Arab world are campaigning, organizing, writing, and working to improve their lives. A landmark conference was held in Cairo at the end of 1999 to assess Qasim Amin's seminal contributions. A century later, the relevance of his work reverberates across class, religious, and ethnic lines. His notoriety clearly overshadowed writings of women who were championing the same causes at the same time, such as Zaynab Fawwaz (1860–1914) or Maryam al-Nahas (1856–1888). Was this because Qasim Amin diligently tied the nationalist project with the reforms of the patriarchal ruling class? Whatever the complex reasons, it is evident that as the Egyptian state took shape, a new gender discourse emerged, and became instrumental in showing that women were crucial to the emerging social development and the nascent national economy.

Today Arab women are entering new fields, and functioning with a new sense of identity. There are more women working in the Arab world than ever before, more engaged in politics, in every scientific domain, and certainly more enrolled in institutions of higher learning. Increasingly, legal, economic, political, social, sexual and reproductive rights and freedoms are sought more as obvious entitlements rather than feminist demands. Significant numbers of women have moved into positions of political power. Many are making their voices heard in the media and throughout the cultural and academic life of their societies, even if they still mostly retain exclusive responsibility for domestic work (which is still unrecognized in official statistics). Although women's roles and expectations in the Arab east have dramatically changed in this past century, we cannot claim that the story is one of simple progress; rather the changes have been uneven, erratic, and reversible, with every gain accompanied by a regression.

It is important therefore to look back to the start of the century, to remember the struggles waged then. Qasim Amin's seminal work of the early 20th century, *Fi tahrir al mar'aa* (The emancipation of women), although still contested in certain Islamist circles today, continues nevertheless to inspire and inform such writers as Nasr Abu-Zeid, whose pivotal work at the end of the same century, "Women in the Discourse of Crisis," is considered a worthy successor of the pioneering Qasim Amin's work (see Chapter 6).

The tired question of the veil, especially in Western media, is possibly put to rest by a courageous writer, Iqbal Barraka, whose most recent study *A New Vision of the Veil* (2003) researches and assesses the matter with great insights. An excerpt of this, is here translated, to share her voice directly (see Chapter 5).

The media increasingly shapes Arab societies. Lives of women are particularly impacted by media, and sometimes in unprecedented ways. Over twenty years ago, the well known and highly acclaimed actor Faten Hamama was instrumental in producing and acting in a hugely successful feature film, *I Want a Solution*, which basically denounced the restrictive divorce laws to which women were subjected, not so much even because of religious dictates, but more by antiquated customary laws. This film ultimately helped bring about the enactment of a new law that, beginning in 2000, gave women the right to ask and obtain *khul'*, a no-contest divorce. Despite much debate, the law is considered an important milestone in women's struggle for more equity (see Chapter 3).

A more recent controversial soap opera, the very successful *Wives of Al Hajj Metwali*, aired in 2001 during the month of Ramadan, ensuring millions of spectators and sparking heated debates in feminist circles throughout the Arab world. How does a man in the 21st century—no matter how lovable, wealthy, and fair in all matters financial, no matter how sanctioned by Shari'a law were his marriages, actually keep four wives and their children and households happy? The soap opera shows the wives and Metwali spending their daily lives together. Each wife has her separate apartment, but all are in the same building owned by the wealthy merchant himself. The soap opera is caustically critical of the women fortune hunters who pursued al Hajj Metwali not only for his charms but especially for his money. Some episodes resorted to exploiting moments of solidarity between the wives, who had bonded inspite of their very different social and educational backgrounds, and the impossible lifestyle of their shared husband. The built-in comic elements that naturally ensued from such unlikely situations were cleverly implemented by a well chosen array of talented actors.

The ending of this highly controversial soap opera was presumably altered in response to the heated debates that it gave rise to in the press, the media in general, in cafés, and especially in the homes of intellectuals and feminists. Al Hajj Metwali finally admitted that it was impossible to sustain his multiple relationships without paying a very high price in health and peace of mind. It also responded to the vociferous protests of feminists, both male and female, who were outraged at the implications of such stances for societies that are actively seeking reforms in matters of personal status.

The fiction and poetry, the films and soap operas, the popular rituals and customs, the political philosophy, the law—all together shape the social, cultural, and political realities of Arab women. The work of the last century that I discuss within this book depicts Arab women exercising new social privileges, discovering new collective identities, and aspiring to the pleasures of a newly discovered modernity.

CHAPTER ONE

Growing up in Egypt at the Turn of the 20th Century

hat was it like to be a young woman of the middle or upper-middle class in Egypt at the beginning of the 20th century? Schools for girls, after all, had been around for quite some time since Al-Sioufiya was founded in 1828. Throughout the Middle East missionaries had opened schools for girls in Beirut and Damascus, as early as 1826. Similar schools cropped up in Palestine and Iraq. While initially these educational institutions catered to the elites, they gradually included children of the growing numbers of civil servants, merchant classes, and professionals. In the 1920s and 30s, many religious orders, as well as secular institutions, had their own schools established, where French, Italian, English, and German were taught as part of the curriculum. It is safe to say that every denomination and religious order was well represented in these schools, Catholic, Protestant as well as secular. (There was a horde of other famous schools for boys such as the renowned Victoria College, Saint Marc, the Jesuits, Les Frères, Lycée Français, and German School.) These were indeed the golden years for these institutions, as they had a free hand in establishing their own rules and regulations, primarily to serve the multitude of foreign communities, but in the process educating elites who eventually played decisive roles in their societies.

There were of course equally prestigious private schools where Arabic was the main language of instruction, such as al-Saniyya al Thanawiyya among others, and where foreign languages were also taught. French institutions such as Le Pensionnat du Sacré Cœur or Les Dames du Sion, as well as the Lycée Français, the English School, Manor House, the American College for Girls, or Saint Clare's College, among many others dedicated to the teaching of girls mushroomed around the country. These schools were, as would be expected, in desirable residential areas like Zamalek (the coveted suburb nestled between two branches of the Nile) and Heliopolis (a fashionable city that was carved out of the desert outside the old city of Cairo), but they were also established in provincial capitals such as Assiyut, Sohag, and Alexandria. This was equally true of the American, British, Italian, and German schools.

But what were some of the social structures that governed the lives of young women in addition to their schooling? What alternative opportunities were offered to these young women? In many ways these schools served the purposes of "finishing" schools, preparing young women to become well educated future wives of the rising bourgeois, merchant, and professional classes. So they were taught, in addition to the regular curriculum, a good dose of "home economics" and arts (painting, music, embroidery, and so forth).

Yet despite the limits of the education, several young women of that generation managed to break away from their pre-ordained destiny as wives first and foremost, and forged brilliant careers with lasting impact on the generations that followed. A list of the women who made their mark on whole subsequent generations reveals that all were the beneficiaries of this elite education. Moufida Abd al Rahman, the famous jurist and lawyer; Saheir al Qalamawy, academic and writer; Laila Doss, founder of charitable foundations; Helena Sidarous, famous gynecologist; Nabawiyya Musa, feminist and educator; Duriyya Shafiq, writer and activist; Amina al Sai'd, journalist and author— these are but a few whose life work paved the way for the thousands who today take for granted their careers in the public and private spheres. These were indeed exceptional women, and they continue to be inspiring role models for millions of young women even today.

But what was life like for the young women who did not achieve these spectacular careers, but who nevertheless had aspirations? For those who might have achieved similar fame had their circumstances permitted? How did these young women view their lives, and negotiate their destinies? How restricted were their lives during that brief period before they committed to marriage? Were they leading confined and restricted lives, as we are led to believe in the many ethnographic, historical, and literary accounts that have appeared in academic circles in the last decades? What were their social lives really like?

Listening to the oral histories of the women who were born in the second and third decade of the 20th century is illuminating. They like to recall these bygone eras, and they help shed a different light on these most interesting decades of the past century. Contrary to the general perception, these young women enjoyed a certain degree of freedom of movement and were deeply involved in both family and social philanthropy.

Lasting friendships were struck, as we can clearly see from the marvelous photographic legacy of that era. These sepia photographs of young women who seemed so enthusiastic to have their pictures taken as they posed for studio photographers, often in group formations with their "best friends," have captured for subsequent generations invaluable insights into the making and workings of these past generations. Personal cameras were not readily available at the time, but luckily we have these portraits, lasting visual testimonies that capture so tellingly the fashions of the time and the mood and tenor of these social relations. These studio portraits taken on occasions such as weddings and birthdays, but also as simply portraits of a time of life: baby pictures, and interestingly also pictures of friends, which were clearly meant to be exchanged as tokens of friendship—souvenirs to be treasured throughout their lives and beyond. These undoubtedly served another more utilitarian purpose, to be also used by "family" matchmakers to find the appropriate groom or bride, since young men as well enjoyed having their portraits taken alone and with friends at the same studios.

I can imagine the social events around which these wonderful portraits were looked at, negotiated, and exchanged. Most likely these young women would breathlessly await the designated day of Istiqbal receptions, or visiting day (a day each week when women would gather for tea at a designated home of one of the members of the group of friends, neighbors, and relatives). "Istiqbal" is a time-honored social custom much like an open house. Here women enjoyed each other's company outside the restrictive circle of the family. This event would be repeated, until it became known, for instance, that every Wednesday the ladies would meet for tea at the home of Latifa, who was

famous for her delicious *khak* (special cookies made of pure butter, honey and different fillings of nuts or dates, made on the occasions of both Muslim and Copt religious feasts, and for new brides). Thursdays were the sole propriety of Aida— none would dare trespass on her turf. Eventually these gatherings, seemingly idle pastimes for the well-to-do, turned into hotbeds of volunteerism for the charitable organizations that became the backbone of the then-budding civil society.

The early beginnings of dozens of foundations started at such meetings, when some of these women sparked with enthusiasm for worthy causes, such as taking care of the needy, sick, or handicapped, organized events and started their long fund raising drives. These were events around which the social life of these societies was organized. They were no less opportunities to show off the hostess's culinary talents (or those of the coveted cook), exchange recipes, and exchange the latest gossip. As the pictures attest, these gatherings were also perfect for examining the latest fashions and studio portraits. Many of these were taken by exceptional artists of portraiture such as Armand, Alban, and Van Leo, many from the talented Armenian community residing in Egypt. Reading these photographic compositions today gives us insight into these exceptionally interesting times of transition and reform. By this time, Qasim Amin's manifesto on the emancipation of women was by now debated in many circles and Ceza Nabarawi and Hoda Sha'arawi were outspoken feminists clamoring for further freedom.

The Istiqbal reception has become a nostalgic tradition that has all but disappeared, the victim of the increasingly harried lifestyle prevalent in Arab societies today. The contemporary working woman cannot afford the bygone luxury of receptions and dedicated visiting days. For one thing, she has lost the moral support and help of the extended family, which in the Arab world, too, is rapidly eroding. Although some are attempting to revive this custom today, in accordance with new dictates of the segregation of the sexes and the return of women to the home called for by extreme-right groups, these customs and their impact have yet to be assessed.

How did a young woman living in the early 20th century negotiate her coming of age, friendships, courtship? I began my research by finding more about my own mother's story. Angele, a Coptic Christian woman, was raised in her much older half-brother's household after being orphaned at a very young age. She had been sent to a boarding school run by French nuns as a tiny pre-schooler when her parents died. When her half-brother became her legal guardian, Angele came to live in a household that, luckily, had a few cousins her age. They soon moved to the fashionable new city Heliopolis, built by the Belgian Baron Empain with wide boulevards and spacious villas. There, she went to another

French high school, where she made lasting friendships with girls from all denominations and ethnicities—Muslim, Jewish, Armenian, Greek, and Italian. Like most eighteen-year-old women at the time, she learned how to play the piano, how to embroider, and took private painting lessons at the Italian school. All artifacts were collected for her trousseau chest. And before long, many of her school friends became her bridesmaids.

Angele's leisure time was mostly spent visiting the neighbors. Since they were close by, she could actually go on her own, or with one of her younger cousins. Of course they had curfew hours to respect, but still they could spend long hours together, at times even visiting the photo-studios to have those wonderful, coveted pictures taken. Perhaps because she was so pretty and orphaned so young, she had a talent for making friends, and was greatly sought after by the young women her age. She carefully collected the many letters and postcards they exchanged (as was the custom), clearly marking them as affectionate keepsakes that speak of lasting friendships. She was very popular, with a lively and fun-loving temperament and a talent for practical jokes. She especially enjoyed April Fool's Day pranks, a habit that remained with her to the very end of her life.

Although my mother was raised in a very traditional and sheltered household, she was well aware of the political turmoil that surrounded her. She recalled seeing the beloved leader of the 1919 Revolution, Saad Zaghloul, in his hometown Zagazig, where she too was born. He was delivering a fiery speech that ended in a skirmish. She never forgot that incident all her life. She recalled that people in the villages believed that Zaghloul's face was mirrored in the full moon and in the cotton flowers in the field, and that as a child she believed the same thing.

Zaghloul was the revered leader of the Wafd Party, which enjoyed over 95 percent support from the voters until his death in 1927, in the golden years of early democratic parliamentary life. (There were, in fact, two competing parties.) The Wafd called for independence from British occupation and the total evacuation of the British troops. Saad Zaghloul remains a symbol of resistance to this day.

When my mother was about fifteen, she heard of the famous women's demonstration that had started in the Coptic Cathedral al Morcossiyya, when Muslim and

Christian women walked through the heart of Cairo with the intent of boycotting British goods in solidarity with the resistance mounted by Saad Zaghloul. She recalled listening to the stories of her uncle Salama Bey, a politician who was exiled with Saad Zaghloul, and eventually went on to become a member of parliament.

What was courtship and marriage like for young women of my mother's milieu? The vast majority, if not all, of the unions were "arranged" by relatives or matchmakers. Yet here's how she recalled her own experience, which must have been fairly representative of many of her friends and relatives. As an eligible, attractive, well educated young woman with all the attributes expected of an early-20th-century woman, she had graduated from a private school with the Brevet (a highly regarded diploma or general certificate) and had studied piano for a number of years. She had also studied art, producing a number of paintings and learning to do pirogravure etching of wood, common in Art Nouveau decorations that to this day grace the walls of many a home. She was about ready at twenty to settle down. But she most certainly was not going to accept any suitor… and there were many to be sure.

Indeed she had refused even to meet a very promising young diplomat who happened to be too short. She had, of course, already seen his photograph at one of those Istiqbal gatherings. As for the elderly wealthy distant cousin, she was adamant not to even look at his pictures, despite the great pressure she faced from her brother and his wife.

She had a harder time refusing the young physician who had just returned from post-graduate medical studies in Vienna and Paris. For she had secretly hoped to go on with her studies at the university like women she had heard of at the Istiqbals—Saheir al Qalamawi, Laila Doss, for example— but her guardian brother would not entertain such a thought.

So she finally accepted the young physician. She had seen several of his pictures, and once their engagement was officially announced she was allowed to meet with him occasionally, in the homes of relatives and common friends. She began to admire and respect her suitor who, in many ways, seemed to fulfill the romantic notions she and many women her age had acquired from their readings of French romances such as *Paul et Virginie* (1787), Bernadin de St-Pierre's chaste and tragic love story, a literary sensation of its age and a precurser to the Romantic movement. Her physician was handsome, courteous, had traveled to study in Vienna and Paris, could speak several languages, and owned a car. She recalled, with a twinkle in her 70-year-old eye, a few drives to her home in Heliopolis—via the Pyramids. These were very long, unchaperoned drives.

Ironically, this would be still frowned upon today in many Arab and Middle Eastern circles. In those days it must have felt very romantic and daring. It seems that young women growing up in the early part of the 20th century in conservative and traditional societies enjoyed a certain degree of freedom— a freedom that is still contested today. Then the freedom reflected, perhaps, the new and energetic historical moment of a rising young nation and a resistance movement against the British occupier. This invigorating mood must have made young people more bold than one might have expected.

My mother had traveled by train by herself to spend a long summer vacation visiting an aunt who was stationed in Palestine, and she recalled with pride this episode of her life, where she enjoyed a degree of independence of movement and dreamed of longer voyages to come.

Her suitor, who had experienced life in Europe, was equally politically engaged and participated in the many demonstrations that persistently demanded the evacuation of the British colonizer. Her seemingly idyllic life of receptions and visitations to photo studios and her happy courtship and marriage were profoundly framed by the atmosphere of political turmoil and new possibility that reigned in the Egypt of the 1930s.

CHAPTER TWO

The Mother of the Bride Frantically Prepares: Egyptian Wedding Customs[1]

*P*opular culture has long been considered a reliable source for understanding society. Even if the diversity and wealth of materials to which a researcher may turn are a part of the difficulty and elusiveness of such endeavors, what better place to examine the roles and differences between men and women than in popular wedding customs. Egyptian contemporary society seems still to be very steeped in its time immemorial customs, traditions, and rituals, at the same time that it is, in other ways, poised for the 21st century.

If we turn to contemporary Egyptian women from different socio-economic, religious, and educational backgrounds, we will note that a good cross-section of these women have adopted new versions of wedding rituals and customs in their wedding celebrations. These practices are often heatedly debated on the pages of newspapers, magazines, as well as the subject of serious academic research conducted at universities and research centers within Egypt itself, and occasionally by anthropologists and sociologists in the West. This essay is more geared to analyzing oral texts (songs and *mawawil*), as well as proverbs and the customs and rituals that give rise to these verbal discourses.

Marriage rituals are performed in both rural and urban settings. Upper class society women are more and more drawn to rediscovering and re-enacting many of these rituals, albeit more as a fashion or fad than as rituals that reflect their actual beliefs. Although there is a fine line between the performance and the belief, not too many studies to my knowledge have attempted to quantify such facts; nor have there been attempts to truly gauge the motivation behind the revival of such customs and rituals in contemporary Egyptian society. We may venture a guess that it is part of the overall tendency to hark back to time-honored traditions that seems to have taken center stage at the start of the 21st century.

This research examines what has steadily become an integral part of wedding ceremonies in middle and upper middle classes in contemporary Egypt. Working classes typically emulate middle class customs, so interestingly they re-appropriate their own ways, via the prism of the middle class.

Terry Eagleton, in his perceptive analysis, situates the discourse in an interesting light. In his study *Against the Grain* he states:

> All (propaganda) or popularization involves the putting of the complex into the simple, but such a move is instantly deconstructive. For if the complex "can" be put into the simple, then it was not as complex as it seemed in the first place. If the simple can be an adequate medium of such complexity, then it cannot after all be as simple as all that. A mutual transference of qualities between simple and complex takes place, forcing us to revise our initial estimate of both terms, and to ponder the possibility that a translation of the one into the otherwise is made possible only by virtue of a secret complicity between them (150).

This "secret complicity," as Eagleton so well puts it, is amply visible between the complex and multi-layered meanings of some of these marriage rituals, and their simplification and use today.

The definitions of "custom" and "tradition" subscribed to in this research are the definitions of sociologists. Customs are produced automatically, to a point when they require no concerted effort.

Tradition is transmitted by word of mouth, or sometimes in writing. This is opposed to *ta'wil*, textually unfounded, or allegorical, interpretations or *sunna*, the tradition that can be traced back to the Prophet. To follow a custom is to follow another without looking for proofs; in many ways, it is an act that is accepted unquestionably. A tradition, on the other hand, is the capacity to enact something consciously, and needs a long period of time to test and try itself, to be reproduced. Traditions, then, are inherently more forceful than customs.

There are still women across the divides who believe that if the bride sucks on a sugar cube during the *Katb al-Kitab* (official signing of the marriage contract), and that same cube is diluted in a glass of water to be subsequently sipped by the unaware groom, a lifelong "sweet" relationship between the newly betrothed is assured.

Another multilayered custom is for the bride to step into a basin of water in which some greenery floats, again sucking on a sugar cube, when she is being dressed on her wedding day. All the while, as she admires herself in a mirror, a female relative, usually the grandmother or aunt, would read verses from the *Quran* if Muslim, or chant prayers or psalms if Christian. The idea behind this endearing ritual is to ensure a fertile (water and greenery) life to the newlyweds, sweet with happiness. The prayers are the obvious blessings, possibly recited as incense is burned, all while the bride looks in the mirror.

The henna-painting ceremony is a time-honored tradition in Egypt and throughout the Arab world. Henna is believed to be a sign of joy. Henna, of course, is not without proponents in the West, though it is primarily used to color hair. Its natural, medicinal properties are appealing in a West that has become interested in all things organic, herbal, and natural. Hundreds of popular songs in the Arab world speak of the joy of wearing henna—a sign of an approaching marriage. The best quality henna comes from the Sudan, and there are wonderful variations on the use and the meaning of the decorations and paintings of the hands, legs, and sometimes faces of brides and grooms. In the Maghreb—that is, Tunisia, Libya, Algeria, and Morocco—the art of henna painting is practiced to perfection. In the Arab Gulf it is equally central as an outward expression of joy. There, brides, and in some cases grooms, wear henna on their hands and feet.

In recent years, the henna painting has become an integral part of the pre-nuptial celebrations for young brides and their whole family and friend's entourage. The well-known pre-nuptial, *laylat al-henna*, usually the night before the wedding, used to be something like a women's version of a bachelor or stag party in the West. It was an evening of celebration, in which the women first prepare the bride for the great wedding ceremony. Part of that preparation was to have her hands and feet decorated with henna. Another was *halawa*, a method of body-waxing believed to have come down from Ancient Egypt and very much practiced to his day. A combination of sugar, water, and lime are cooked in a special way and used to clean the excess hairs off different parts of the body. Today, Fifth Avenue and Rodeo Drive beauty salons boast of having this procedure done at hefty prices.

Beauty salons in Egypt, too, now offer these services, and every young woman learns while growing up the secrets of perfecting this beautifying secret. One can also purchase a ready-made formula from drugstores, which travels well. In recent years, the proliferating Body Shops throughout major cities carry variations on this beautifying product, such as loofahs and pumice stones.

A *ballana* was a professional woman who visited ladies of society once a week to help bathe them, using a woolen glove and a form of massage that approximated abrasion, or peeling. I still recall these weekly events I experienced as a very young child, and distinctly remember that navy blue woolen glove. The *ballana* was a coveted position, for obviously she was introduced to the most intimate circle of a household, with all the implications that she could divulge secrets about her employers. They were implicitly sworn to secrecy and were valued for their discretion, although one can imagine the infinite possibilities and consequences of divulging secrets to a rival household. *Ballanas* also doubled as matchmakers, praising the beauty of their client to prospective mother-in-laws. Public beauty salons, which began offering some of the services previously performed by the *ballana*, gradually put an end to those intimate visitations and all the social structures that flourished around her. Additionally, the fancy spas frequented by the rich and famous have in many ways today replaced the services of the *ballana*, and the function, too, of the traditional public Turkish baths, steam baths much more accessible to large segments of society in the past.

The henna ceremony has become today very much a rehearsal wedding in every sense of the word. Families outdo themselves trying to make this a memorable event, and it has evolved from its roots as an intimate family gathering exclusively for women. Today, in the urban middle classes it has become a full-fledged occasion.

This may very well be one of the reasons why young people are under greater and greater stress when unable to live up to these burdensome expenses. In addition, there is the *mahr* and *shabka* dowry paid by the groom, and the wedding rings and perhaps even other gold jewelry. *Mahr* has consistently been misrepresented in Western sources as the "bride price." It is not that; it is technically meant as almost an insurance policy fo the bride, along with the *mua'khar al saddak*, or the arrears as it were, in cases of divorce. In a Muslim marriage contract, the *mahr* has to be stated, even if it is a symbolic sum of money. The *mahr* is very often used by the bride and her family to furnish the new home the couple will share. The value of the *mahr* is commensurate, of course, with the standing of the families involved. Even to this day, marriage is very much the union of two families. Today, when the couple choose each other by themselves (and this is becoming more the norm than the exception), the families still come together to discuss more directly the mechanics of these matters.

The *mu'akhar* is more of a guarantee in case things don't work out. In that spirit it can be a wonderful built-in mechanism to ensure the well-being of the woman. In a sense it is a form of pre-nuptial agreement, where sometimes things are spelled out in much more detail. For instance, the well known *issma bi yiddi al arous*, is a clause that every Muslim woman can insist on including in the marriage contract, which guarantees that she can ask for a divorce. Usually this was a privilege given to upper-class women who married sometimes "beneath" their class. Hence, they carried a title often mentioned before their names. For instance, the wife of the famous Wafdist leader Mustapha al-Nahas, was known as Sahibat al-Isma, Zaynab al-Wakil. Grooms are traditionally responsible for all expenses, from paying the services of the *ma'zun*, the cleric who performs wedding contracts (or for Christians, the rental of church and priests' services), to the reception expenses, to the wedding rings, of course, and all other extra and miscellaneous incidentals.

The wedding receptions are becoming increasingly onerous and in many ways outrageous. Throughout the Arab world, these customs are beginning to be questioned. For instance, in the Gulf countries, fear is growing that more and more women may have to face a life of spinsterhood because young men are finding it increasingly impossible to provide the requisite *mahr* and expenses of setting themselves up properly. That is why many of them turn to "foreign" brides either from the other Arab countries, or more recently from Asian Muslim countries, such as Indonesia, Malaysia, and the Philippines. This is creating much controversy within these societies. In other countries such as Egypt, Syria, and Lebanon, young men seek expatriation at great personal sacrifice, mostly to be able to "afford" a wife, which includes buying an apartment and footing the expensive bill of a wedding and its accoutrements. Very often, relationships founder because the young man stays away too long and is unable to come up with the necessary, compulsory expenses. Hence the mail to the "Dear Abbie's" of the Arab world is filled with letters signed "Broken heart," or "Help—tell me what to do." Most complaints are about the difficulty of getting together for young people. The complaints have become so widespread that the debate in the media is becoming more openly critical of these accepted norms.

In recent years, television soap operas and sitcoms virtually all address these nagging questions, which are exacerbating the discontent among the youth (who incidentally comprise over half of the population in these societies). A growing number of feature films with leading actors have addressed these questions in very realistic and sometimes poignant terms. The well-known feature film, *Intabihou ayuha al Saada* (Gentlemen Beware), was one of the first and most effective of such treatments. In it, a university professor falls in love with a college student and they get engaged. He is unable, though, to come up with the necessary sums of money to buy or even rent a decent apartment. Meanwhile, the mother (proverbially in Arab society and in such representations), becomes more and more unhappy with the situation, putting tremendous pressure on her daughter. The garbage collector snubbed by the philosophy professor and the young woman, very quickly becomes a millionaire selling garbage, builds a highrise and offers the young couple the possibility of renting a place in the unfinished building. Of course, they have to come up with the necessary money to finish the apartment—to put in, for example, a bathroom, kitchen, tiles, electricity, and so forth, and of course furnish the apartment when it is all done. Predictably he is unable to do it all on his meager university salary. The unbelievable happens: the garbage collector proposes to the beautiful young woman, who becomes his second wife under pressure from her nagging mother. The last scene is the young woman in her expensive wedding gown being serenaded down the proverbial staircase in the villa of the nouveau rich garbage collector. (Egyptian cinema has perpetrated a myth of what it is to be wealthy, and having a villa with a winding staircase has always been the semiotic equivalent of this coveted wealth. The hundreds of times that the famous heroines—actresses such as Fatin Hammama, Shaddia, Magda—have either swooned, been carried up the stairs à la Rhett Butler in *Gone With the Wind*, or been serenaded as they descend on their wedding day is indeed a phenomenon that ought to be studied more closely). In this case it was the beautiful Souad Hosni and the handsome Hussein Fahmy who were the star-crossed lovers, while the astute Mahmoud Yassin was perfect in impersonating the social climbing garbage collector. *Gentlemen Beware* and numerous other feature films have elaborated on this central dilemma of Arab youth of a certain class today. None to my mind drove the lesson home so forcefully.

With the implications of this situation in mind, I will take some measure of the ceremonies, festivities, and especially texts of *mawawil* (songs) performed at these weddings. Though these examples are taken from events I have attended in the last couple of years, for the sake of the privacy of my relatives and friends, I have used fictitious names.

Mounira, a young Coptic woman whose parents were born in the Sudan, was given an extraordinary traditional henna ceremony that was a combination of Egyptian and Sudanese rituals. The very elaborate henna painting session lasted virtually 24 hours. Mounira's individual painting session lasted at least four hours, during which Santouna, a famous Sudanese henna painter, completely covered the forearms and legs of the pretty bride with very elaborate floral designs, while the woman's very large extended family sang, burned incense, danced to enticing rhythms, and shared delicious food in her family's home. The mother of the bride, followed by the future mother-in-law, and—in descending order of kinship importance—the other women, got their arms or hands or ankles painted. By nighttime, a large gathering of both men and women joined in a more formal dinner. The groom and his brothers had henna painted on their heels and hands. All joined in dancing and singing, eating and drinking and being merry.

This had been preceded by the bride being immersed in imported ointments from the Sudan, a form of mud/weed bath while some aunts sang traditional songs. Later, the hairdresser came to the home and gave her a beautiful upswept hairstyle. The next day was yet another henna celebration, which was actually a sit-down dinner at a fancy restaurant; there the young bride wore a very beautiful cocktail dress and sat on a *kosha* (throne) decked in flowers. After the sumptuous dinner, the bride surprised everyone present by donning a traditional Sudanese costume and performing a beautiful dance carrying some incense and dancing with her groom. Many later joined in this very festive and joyous ritual. The henna painter led the chorus of traditional songs. The traditional "oriental" dancer, and then both the groom and the bride, and the guests danced, as has become the custom now at weddings.

Another henna ceremony was less elaborate, with the intimate circle of friends and family gathered to sing and dance and rehearse the next day's expected events. The bride's parents, incidentally, traditionally underwrite the henna ceremony—much as in the West, a groom's family will pay for the rehearsal dinner. In a sense, it is a way of sharing the expenses, or in some cases it is a way for upmanship to express itself, as when sometimes the henna ceremony, especially if it is an upper class society, often outshines the wedding reception, which is supposed to be the crowning event.

The last two decades or so have witnessed some very radical innovations, which are clearly imports from the Gulf countries. It is becoming more and more acceptable, for example, that the grooms pay for the bride's wedding gown. A more disconcerting innovation harkens back to a distant past: the sexes are segregated for the actual festivities. This too is very much an import from Gulf society, and it seems to have taken root at least in some conservative circles. Apparently even in North America Arab women from conservative religious backgrounds prefer to celebrate with the bride among themselves, wearing their low-cut dresses, tight shifts, as well as fancy hairdos and makeup, presumably because in mixed company they would not be able to to "show off" their fancy clothes. So, for a few hours, daily reality is suspended, and segregation imposed, if only to exhibit one's wares to one's peers. Women together are also presumably less inhibited to express themselves by signing and dancing. This is not the norm in Egypt or elsewhere, but it is becoming more acceptable and deserves to be assessed, for it is a rather disturbing development with possible dire consequences. It is a re-invention of harem days, but without the complex structures and sophisticated rationale that governed harems.

Another more interesting innovation is the role of the mosque in becoming, like the church, the venue for the marriage ceremony, *Katb al-Kitab*. More and more Muslims in North America are adopting this innovation. It is also becoming an accepted custom in Egypt. Even wedding invitations now include beautiful verses from the *Quran* similar to the quotes from the Gospels and Bible often included in wedding invitations.

The wedding *zaffa* (parade) has become an extremely elaborate happening. Today, there is a successful attempt, not only at re-enacting the traditional *zaffa*, but also at reviving certain regional ones. So, for instance, the *zaffa Dumiyattiyya*, coming from Damietta in the Nile Delta, has become almost a staple of the very fancy weddings held at the best hotels, such as the Intercontinental Hilton or Marriott in either Cairo or Alexandria. The Alexandrian *zaffa* is equally popular. The *zaffa Dumiyattiyya* has the men wearing uniforms in white and red, with very large drums and tambourines singing and dancing for the groom and bride. Some of the lyrics of these very loud and sometimes (possibly intentionally) unintelligible words are meant to excite the bride and groom, to ensure a passionate consummation on their wedding night. The words are rather licentious, hedonistic in content, but not without general wisdom. Many Western educated couples shun such overtly lewd expressions of joy or ritual. Many opt not to have a *zaffa*, and others claim religious sanctions (both Christian and Muslim) against having a belly dancer as part of the entertainment.

x.⚬⚬⚬.x

Textual analyses of some of these lyrics can shed light on the mores, customs, and traditions—and on the openness and lack of inhibitions in some classes of society. These lyrics are imports from the countryside to urban centers, and perhaps the agricultural milieu has always been much less inhibited in expressing matters of sex and love.

A woman's body and its beauty are undoubtedly the focal point for most of these lyrics:

> *Abu Sinna Luli Ya ard Ihrussi ma'aliki*
> Oh you with pearl teeth, Oh ground protect those who tread upon you.
> *Idahrag wa igri ya rummman, minn gwaa luli ya rummman.*
> Frolic and roll, Oh pomegranate, your insides are pearls, oh pomegranate.[2]

Pomegranates are of course, symbolic of a woman's breasts, and in general a cherished fruit.

Another lyric is more graphic and almost re-enacts foreplay and the consummation of the sexual act.

> *Hatt iddu alla sha'ri, Yamma ya sha'ri*
> He put his hand, oh mother on my hair
> *Ya Habbib 'allbitaht shiawiyya*
> Love of my heart, just lower your touch a bit
> *Hatt iddu all ourti Ya amma ya ourti*
> He placed his hand on my forehead mother on my fore
> *Ya Habbib 'allbitaht shiwayya*
> Love of my heart, just lower your touch a tiny bit
> *Hatt iddu alla bouki*
> He placed his hand on my mouth
> *Hatt iddu alla sidri*
> He placed his hand on my chest...

The lyric proceeds to the navel and beyond, though the uninhibited lyrics are often incomprehensible because of the loud drum beating accompanying them, as well as the general atmosphere of the festivities.

Another explicitly lyric goes as follows:

> *Ya mikatta' ya 'amis el noum*
> The nightgown is all shredded
> *Y mibahdil shubban al-youm*
> And this drives the young men crazy

The lyric goes on to say:

He laid his hair on mine, that has stolen sleep away from his eyes
He placed his cheek on my cheek, and stole sleep from my eyes.
Oh you who drive the young men berserk
He placed his mouth on my mouth, and stole sleep from my eyes
He placed his belly on my belly, and stole sleep from my eyes
He placed his *eissa* on my *moussa*, and now truly sleep has overcome me.

This rising crescendo of the song, and its escalating meanings, are accentuated by the refrain. Incidentally, it is common to refer to the beloved (woman or man) using the masculine form. This is quite possibly a literary device to avoid being sanctioned. Another aspect of such lyrics is the clever choice of rhyming schemes, which lend themselves to plays on words, innuendo, and double entendre.

A wedding procession lyric, very much from the rural countryside:

Yalli 'alla al-tira'a hawid al malih
 O you who are by the riverbank, bringing over the pretty one (or salty one)
Min li-bak fih laylt imbarrih.
 My hair hurts from your playing with it last night.

Here, note the rhyming alliteration of "*malih*" (salty) and "*imbarrih*" (last night). The lyric proceeds to inventory as it were the different parts of the body, using the same routine. So, it is the forehead, followed by the cheeks, by the lips, the chest/breasts, the side, and culminates by stating that it hurts because of "sleeping" last night. The river referred to as "*malih*" actually refers to the sea (salt water), and the inference is that the sea is stormier—more passionate—than a dreamy, serene stream or river.

So the groom stands, holding hands with his bedecked bride, while the singers serenade them with these lyrics and the womenfolk ululate (the special way of expressing joy). Working class people then drive off in cars, honking their way to the shrine (*maqam*) of their favorite holy man or woman (*awila*). Once there, they circle the shrine seven times, for good luck.

A vast repertoire of folk lyrics has become popular with almost all socio-economic classes, supported by a proliferation of regional groups such as those from Damietta or Alexandria. *Zaffas* themselves seem responsible for this widespread, almost faddish, revival. Luckily, an important legacy that was in danger of disappearing is being preserved. This revival has spurred new songwriters to create variations on the themes discussed above. Often, not surprisingly, the new songs are more in tune with new and pressing social realities and the changing rhythms of society. Some of these lyrics are more thoughtful, often narrating dramatic vignettes, and are put to very enticing music, which lends itself to quick memorization by both performers and listeners.

"'Yuun Bahiyya" (Bahiyya's Eyes) interpreted by Muhammad al'Izabbii, is one such narrative. It basically speaks of the beauty of Bahiyya's eyes, and how this beauty was the envy of the whole village, and her fame spread far and wide to the ends of the earth. The singer warns her to remain behind closed doors, lest she is accused of being a provocative flirt. Here we must note that traditionally the name "Bahiyya" has always been allegorical for Egypt. One can speculate, then, on the political implications of representing Egypt as the beautiful, coveted one.

> 'Yuun Bahiyya
> Ruddi al hibban ya Bahiyya
>   Bahiyya closes the doors
> Wa Ya Bahiyya wi khabirini malhum bikki il layymin
>   Bahiyya tell me why are you the envy of all
> Di uyunik bil huz malyaninin
>   Your eyes are filled with sadness

Kul magarih al hawa bi yullu hiyya Bahiyya
All those who succumbed to the pains of love blame Bahiyya
Zallamu il biny, wi kull il hikkayya 'yun Bahiyya
They unfairly accused her, and all because of her beautiful eyes
Dari il 'uyuun, la il nass yihsiduki
Hide those eyes, lest you be envied, and given the evil eye
Willi fi 'iniha ma la'ash mawadda
Since they found no encouragement from her
Zalamu il sabiyya, wi rah wi aal
They unfairly accused her of being a flirt
Hiyya malahash aziz wa la habib
Though in fact, she has no dear one, she has no lover
'Uynha ti'til wa mlahash dawa
Her eyes can kill you with their beauty and there is no cure
    from them
Zalamu il binaya wi kull il hikkaya 'uyun Bahiyya
They falsely accused her, and all because of her eyes
Husn al sabiyya, wa yama yama kull al wilad fi akher il balad,
    'ishuq al Bahiyya
All the boys, all over the country, to the end of the earth
    have fallen in love with Bahiyya
Kull al hisan hasadu al sabiyya
All the beautiful lasses have envied her.

We can note here, the alliterations and their effectiveness. Bahiyya, which can also mean beautiful, rhymes with *sabiyya* (lass); *hissan* (beautiful) also rhymes with bibban, which means doors, behind which she is advised to hide. She is also advised to "hide" her eyes, her treasures too (*dari al'uyun*).

Egypt is always a beautiful woman. Egyptian women have been referred to as flirtatious, beautiful, and coveted, from the earliest of times, and especially from the Islamic conquest. 'Amr Ibn al'Aas, who conquered Egypt in 642 CE is said to have summarized his views of Egypt in these succinct lines, not very complimentary all in all, but somehow the lines pertaining to women seem to have stuck for all these centuries, another internal stereotype, perhaps:

Nisa'uha lu'aab
    its women are flirtatious
rijaluha 'ajab

its men are strange
wa al ard liman ghalab
and the land to whomsoever can conquer it

Some believe that "strange" was a reference to bilharzioses, a disease that caused bleeding and was endemic to the Egyptian fellah. The last line referred to a time when Egypt was indeed vulnerable, at the end of the decadent rule of Dioclietian.

A light-hearted song, often repeated at weddings again has the countryside as a setting. A dialogue between a chorus of village girls and the *'umda* (mayor of the village). Basically, the lasses are reporting to the *'umda*, who happens to be the father of Himida, the village bully, that his son and his friends (the effendis) the city boys, have annoyed, even accosted Hamida, a village girl. They appeal to him to restrain his son Himida (or else declare his serious intentions, and ask for Hamida's hand in marriage—after all, she is a beautiful lass, with an impeccable reputation.) The lyrics are most charming. The chorus sings the events, and the *'umda*, in his proverbial commanding voice merely takes in the facts, and hums as if he were very much in control. The chorus narrates the simple, flirtatious events. Himida and his friends from the city (*effendiyya*) threw tangerines (*ustafindiyya*) on her chest, provoking her to respond. (We note here again, the charming alliteration and rhyme scheme). Her friends presumably are there to shield her from anything that would blemish her reputation, (*sharraf*) or honor, and so the song goes.

> *Ya hadritt al 'umda, Himida ibnak hadifni bistafindiyya,*
> Mr. Mayor, your son Himida threw tangerines at me
> *Wissihabu dihku 'laffandiyya*
> His friends the city boys laughed at her,
> *Yirdik ya 'umda 'ashan ibn 'umda*
> Is this fair—is it because he is the son of a *'umda*?
> *Abu Himida matihush Himida*
> O father of Himida, restrain your son Himida
> *'Uyun Hamida wi Shihraha Hamida hilwa wi sirritha hilwa fi*

al ballad
  Hamida has enticing eyes. Hamida is pretty, and has a good
reputation.
*Ihna ghallaba wa mahnash ghallaba insif al ghallaba sharraf al
sabiyya*
  We may be poor, but we are not helpless poor...

Many of these lyrics, as the two above, are based on
formulaic givens. There is the beautiful girl, who is either
flirtatious by nature, or falsely accused because of her beauty,
because she would not succumb to her detractors. There is
always honor to be protected, and usually a sense of unfair
play. Yet, the earlier lyrics were quite uninhibited, open, and
even licentious by puritanical standards.

We must remember to situate these lyrics within the
context of very lavish wedding receptions, generally enacted
for the middle and upper-middle classes. These would only
be an introductory part of the entertainment, which in some
cases would go on to the wee hours of the night, perhaps
with famous singers and dancers. A band or disc jockey
might provide a Western interlude; other receptions feature
floorshows of flamenco or Russian mazurka. (In recent years,
Russian belly dancers have flooded the market, to the dismay
of the indigenous dancers. Presumably, the Russians ask for
much less money). We have to imagine, also, the elaborate
setting at the hotels, particularly the flower arrangements,
which may run to thousands of dollars. There are also many
variations on the grand entrance of the bride. In recent years,
there seems to be no limit to the imagination and expense
never seems to be an issue. Some of these elaborate
productions could rival Broadway or Hollywood in the
special effects. Laser beams synchronized, for instance, with
Verdi's *Aida*. The bride ushered in a replica of the Pharoanic
chariot pulled by a bevy of young men dressed in the
appropriate garb, naked torsos and all. And always, the
inevitable laser show highlighting the ten-story wedding
cake. Lights go off, and laser beams focus attention on the

cake, perhaps with romantic doves let loose on the stage in a cloud of smoke.

One of the more bizarre and eccentric weddings to hit the scene took place in the summer of 1997. Magazines and newspapers spoke of the "Mad Mad Wedding." Guests were asked to come in disguise, as if it were Halloween or Mardi Gras. Elaborate, beautiful masks were made available to guests. The t-shirt clad bride and groom entered riding bicycles. Afterwords, they changed to a traditional tuxedo and elaborate wedding gown, in order to make their second entrance. This time, the mother of the bride was pushed in on an elevated float, and after singing a well-known song about a mother's love for her daughter, her Marie Antoinette dress opened up to reveal... her daughter. It was almost like giving birth in public, but to her daughter in full regalia. The veil was lit with flickering bulbs and then the Russian dancers led her in the wedding procession to her groom. Finally, both the groom and the bride were set on a floating huge balloon in the shape of red lips. Their finale was even more eccentric. They exited on a bulldozer. (They were both civil engineers and the father of the bride was a very successful contractor).

Of course, these are by no means average weddings. Yet these examples give an idea of the variety and the recent changes in a society that is in many ways searching for a new identity. A society that is, on the one hand, anxious to maintain its authenticity, and on the other hand, not shy to experiment, even to the point of the absurd. Incidentally, people seemed to be having a grand time. Women wearing the proverbial *hijab* (veil) were happy to don masks instead. Weddings are, as in all societies, pivotal. In a country like Egypt, they are still very much family affairs—almost more about the union of two families than anything else, even if the bride and groom chose each other on their own. Deciding how to celebrate, then, becomes a matter of declaring who the families are and what their standing is in society. In some cases, they revert to one-upmanship, and in nearly all cases it becomes a stressful, competitive, yet very much awaited, event. Yet interestingly, across the board, whatever the status of the families, many of the same lyrics would be sung.

And there are popular expressions about love and marriage, too, that straddle the classes. The saying alluded to in the title of this chapter, *Ill'arousa li'll 'ariss wa al garyy li'll ma'taiss*, is translated roughly as follows: A bride and groom have a life full of love, while their family runs around frantically preparing for the wedding celebration. Of course such a saying—which may seem very familiar in the West as well—arose because of the elaborate, time-consuming, and even exhausting, traditions involved in the wedding. And tradition had it that the mother of the bride and her female relatives would do all of the wedding arrangements. This saying applies to other situations, too: whenever some people do all the work behind the scene and others take the credit or benefit in one way or another. The expression *Zayy umm al-aroussa fadia wi mashghulla* was also inspired by the mother-of-the-bride's frantic running around: "Like the mother of the bride, carefree and overly busy." This saying, again, applies to anyone who pretends to be very busy, but at the same time seems to have nothing to do.

The skeptics offer these sayings: *Aidit al khazana walla al gawazza al nhadama* (Better remain within one's room, than be miserably married). Or, as the French so rightly say, *Il vaut mieux être seul que mal accompagné* (Better to remain alone than be in bad company). But here, finally, is a well-known proverb that says it all, for people will continue to marry, however much their weddings change: *Dhill rajil walla dhil haitt* (Better the shadow of a man, than the shadow of a wall.)

CHAPTER THREE

I Want a Solution: Films and Social Change

*A*n epoch-making feature film, *I Want a Solution*, created such controversy at the time of its release in 1974 that its reverberations continue to this day. At the dawn of the 21st century, one can easily say that its aftershocks are still being felt, and some would venture to claim that the highly controversial laws enacted concerning *Khul'*, or the right of women to ask for a no-fault divorce and forfeit all their rights to any form of compensation, dowry, alimony, or otherwise, is the direct consequence of this extraordinary film.

The story behind this drama (or one can say docudrama, since it enacted a true story) is itself a tale of women empowering themselves. Silver screen legend Faten Hamama, sometimes called the First Lady of Arab Cinema, the beloved diva of millions for over three-quarters of a century and still active, unveiled the circumstances behind the making of this defining film in Egyptian women's history. She mentioned in an interview (29 May 2000) with the TV personality, Moufid Fawzy, how the idea came about. Apparently at a social gathering the highly respected journalist Amina al-Said, editor-in-chief of the very popular and influential women's weekly, *Hawa* (Eve), told the very touching story of a woman who, like a million others, was one day informed by her husband that she had to leave her comfortable life as the wife of an executive, for he had decided to marry a younger woman. She had to accept a one-year alimony payment and fend for herself for the rest of her life. As a childless woman, she had no option but to seek some form of employment. Having never worked before in her life and having no living relatives who might have helped her, she ended up supporting herself by working as a janitor at a day-care center.

Faten Hamama was apparently extremely disturbed by this story, and after a sleepless night, she contacted her friend and schoolmate, Husn Shah, a writer and a lawyer, and urged her to investigate the topic from a legal point of view. Husn Shah diligently went about her task and spent quite some time in the law courts recording the heart-breaking cases of women from across the socio-economic spectrum. She discovered scores of poignant stories. Faten Hamama subsequently commissioned her to write a script, which became the drama that touched the hearts and minds of millions, and after 26 years, the law changed.

With her story and facts in hand, Faten Hamama first had the difficult task of convincing male directors and producers of their importance. They initially were "amused" by the story and inclined to dismiss it. Upon her insistence, they went reluctantly to visit some courts of personal status and found incredible material for what has become one of the most popular films of the second half of the 20th century.

The thrust of the dramatic action of the film *I Want a Solution* centered on the equally poignant true story of a tyrannical Egyptian diplomat who refused to divorce his wife and kept her in the House of Obedience (*Bayt al-Taa'aa*). This antiquated institution forced his dissident wife to live under his roof and accept his imposed conjugal advances, intolerable as they may have seemed. In the dramatized version, Faten Hamama was in a worse bind since she had to give up her beloved son. The intransigent husband, superbly portrayed by the handsome Roushdy Abaza, took his vengeance by repudiating her, not divorcing her, thus preventing her from re-marrying. In the film, she might have remarried an attractive, sensitive, and artistic friend of her brother's. But she was forced to remain unmarried—in her words, like a property that was likened to a *waqf* (charitable property), to be set free. Indeed the real life story upon which the film was modeled only unraveled last year when the diplomat finally died, setting free his wife.

Amina Risk forcefully portrayed the role of the older childless woman unjustly divorced by her husband and left to fend for herself in the merciless courts. A very famous actress on the stage and screen, Risk made a brief but unforgettable appearance in the film, highlighting the helplessness of women, young or old, when faced by such unjust laws.

The film also portrayed a poor woman who could only achieve some form of justice by fakery: she breaks a water jug on her own head and appears before the judge bleeding and in tears, claiming it was her husband's cruelty. This provided a moment of comic relief, since for a brief moment, the man was the victim, but neverthess it was a wonderful portrayal of the desperate solutions poverty provokes. The film's focus on a group of women separated by class, age, and educational background is what makes it so important. Those wide ranges of voices needed to be heard, and their different perspectives benefited the audience. The visibility of contradictory ideas and awareness of conflicting positions helped bring the case of "repudiated" women to the forefront. The film thus makes an across-the-board condemnation of the conditions under which women from all classes live, and it touched millions, who saw themselves, or sympathized with their sisters, mothers, or friends.

Before and since this film, there have been scores of soap operas, radio shows, and more feature films that have treated this topic, but none as forcefully as *I Want a Solution*. Many people believe that the film was even present in the minds of the legislators when they sat down to wrestle with the thorny laws of *Khul'*. Here was a case where the media was not merely representing reality, but helping change it. In this case, the media produced meaning through an interaction between text, reader, and viewer. There is not, however, a simple relationship between film and social change.

Here we are invited to dig beneath the text's surface and explore its structures to uncover the film's sociological stances. *I Want a Solution* clearly uses parallelisms in presenting the narratives of the three women from three different classes. The story of the baladi working-class mother who survives by her wits, and ends up marrying an "ambulance-chaser" of a lawyer, provides comic relief in an otherwise melodramatic movie. The older woman, though, disappears, and we learn that she died without getting any retribution: a chilling reminder that often happy endings do not come. Yet two of the three women manage to circumvent the time-worn customs, and the portrayal of this, combined with the film's implicit denunciation of Arab machismo and double standards, was a forceful movement from silence, a defining step toward change for all women.

x.☙❧.x

The heated debate over the Personal Status Procedure Law in the People's Assembly raised the alarming specter of broken families and soaring crime. The legislation, finally approved by the Assembly, declared that it was aimed at facilitating and speeding up litigation in personal status disputes, particularly divorce. Women have the right to a court divorce, irrespective of her husband's consent, if she forgoes her financial rights (the much debated *Khul'*), the legal mechanism that would have saved so much grief for our film heroine and the real woman who inspired the film. Finally: the solution was found, at the dawn of the 21st century. Of course, it is not so simple as all that. Some have argued that the new law serves men's interests more than women's, and that it should not be used, because it stands in the way of genuine equality (for the woman, after all, is required to forfeit her economic rights to achieve the right of divorce).

The Grand Imam of Al-Azhar, the highest religious authority in Islam, Sheikh Tantawi, affirmed that the bill has been revised to comply fully with Sharia. The Islamic Research Academy, made up of forty scholars, approved Khul' by a majority vote. There are six reasons a woman can apply for a divorce without giving up her financial rights. Injury or harm is the major one, but the latter is very hard to prove to a judge. Some contend that many applications for divorce are being rejected simply because women are unable to talk about their personal relations with their husbands before male judges. This, of course, brings to the fore another very controversial matter: the appointment of female judges in Personal Status Courts. Women already serve as judges in civil government management courts that deal with cases of corruption, embezzlement, and misuse of public funds. The argument for the appointment of female judges across the board is further reinforced by the fact that neighboring Tunisia and Jordan have de facto female judges; why not Egypt? As it stands now, even a woman's right to travel without the permission of her husband has been denied by courts.

The *urfi* (unregistered marriage contract) remains one of the thorniest social phenomenons to have plagued Egyptian society in the last decade of the 20th century. A media blitz took over the topic, and pundits of every shape and ilk continue to discuss its validity and legality from a religious perspective. The unauthorized "signed" piece of paper between two consenting adults is dismissed as non-binding and carries no weight in the court of law when claiming inheritance or different forms of alimony, child support, etc.

Urfi marriages are now being called in the media secret unions whose sole reason is to legitimize sexual relations in the eyes of the couple. Indeed Sheikh Kotb, an articulate member of the Assembly of Azhar Scholars has unequivocally condemned this growing phenomenon, especially among university students. The consensus among sociologists as well as religious scholars is that since the marriage contract is by definition a public act that needs the representation of a male relative at the time of signing the contract (plus a traditional two witnesses), an *urfi* marriage is void and non-binding, and many think, should be penalized.

In trying to understand the origins of this new social behavior, which seems to be spreading like brushfire, especially across university campuses, researchers have concluded that socio-economic pressures are forcing young adults to find accommodating temporary solutions to their rising frustrations in finding adequate affordable housing, starting families because of the unrealistic demands of parents for *mahr* and all the other deeply entrenched customs and traditions. In a highly conservative atmosphere that still considers any form of relationships outside marriage as utterly taboo, young people have found their own mechanisms for bypassing the restrictive measures that have only become more confining in recent decades. Moreover, the association of this behavior with outlawed Islamic groups, who have instituted these *urfi* marriages for their followers since the early 1980s, has added a thicker cloud over what is dismissed as merely a means of satisfying urgent sexual desires. It is interesting to note that in all these discussions no mention is made of the Shi'ite custom of *mutaa* marriages (marriages of pleasure), temporary, non-binding unions for the specific purpose of sexual gratification.

The sociologists bemoan the fact that young women are ill-advised since they knowingly or unknowingly forfeit their legal rights, and in addition stand to lose so much more since they may have to face the lonely solution of having dangerous abortions performed if pregnancies result from these illicit relationships. There seems to be a well mounted campaign against *urfi* marriages with very little else offered as an alternative to the pressing needs of these young people who are caught at the crossroads of change.

x.❦.x

A century ago, Qasim Amin and his vociferous followers clamored for the emancipation of women and their right to equal education, following in the footsteps of earlier great reformers, such as Muhammad Abdu and Rifaa Rafi' al-Tahtawi. Today, women in Egypt and the rest of the Arab world grapple with more complex dimensions of oppression, questions that border on the political, social, personal, philosophical, religious, and ethical, in addition to the unsolved endemic problem of illiteracy and its accompanying baggage of inherited backwardness.

To respond more readily to these feminist debates, the Egyptian government has instituted a National Council for Women, which reports directly to Egypt's president. The First Lady heads the council, with its selective membership of mostly prominent women and some men who are re-drawing the map for the continued struggle for women's emancipation. The monumental task facing this new institution is that no one issue can be understood or solved in isolation, for changes have a cumulative effect, and progress in one area can be both dependent upon and a precondition for progress in others. The concept of patriarchy is being timidly challenged and seen not merely as a private concern but as part of a process through which dominant relations of power are reflected or challenged.

Another highly popular soap opera that mesmerized audiences during the month of Ramadan (1999–2000) and galvanized public opinion in a wave of nostalgia for "*al-zaman al-gamil*" (the beautiful era) was the soap opera *Umm Kulthum*. It depicted the life and times of that quintessential diva, that unique personality and unmatched Arab voice of the 20th century. A very successful documentary based on the research of Virginia Danielson had already introduced Umm Kulthum, this singer who was so much more, to American audiences. French television had produced a highly acclaimed documentary, too, and scores of books about her have been written since her death in 1971.

But nothing seems to have touched the audiences more than this soap opera, directed by a woman, Inam Muhammad Aly and written by Ni'mat Fouad. Once more a group of woman together created a highly successful production. The representation of this beloved idol boosted the sales of her songs and recordings among the generation weaned on 'Amr Diab, Madonna, and Michael Jackson, too young to have experienced Umm Kulthum in her day. The show successfully portrayed a woman rising from the rural hamlet of Tamay al-Zahiriyya to achieve the greatest fame. At her feet, the rulers and potentates of several generations were prostrate. She was a most powerful role model, unique, true of her kind, and her legacy remains for today's disillusioned generation, many of whom have had nothing but defeat and frustrated aspirations, and now face a globalization that threatens to rip away their sense of identity.

The sensitive director, Inam Muhammad Aly, and very talented actress Sabrine must be credited with the success of this adaptation of Umm Kulthum's life. Is it surprising that it was the collaboration of a talented group of women that brought this important woman's story to television? Umm Kulthum's life has much to tell young women today. She was a woman who managed to remain within the confines of her conservative background, yet defy norms and taboos by remaining single for the better part of her life. When she did choose a partner, she was able to do so from a large group of persistent suitors, which rant the gamut from royalty to simple peasants. She chose the best of the best when it came to selecting her poets, composers, and members of her orchestra. Her great managerial talents at orchestrating teamwork are even successfully portrayed here. Of course, not everyone can hope to have a voice as divine as Umm Kulthum's, but her sharp intelligence and ability to stretch the received destiny of "woman" are inspirations to us all.

These vibrant works—the film and the TV show—were both politically and sociologically explosive. In different ways they struck at the malaise that periodically grips our societies. *I Want a Solution* unleashed heated debates within feminist circles, and managed to instigate change, finally, years later. The Umm Kulthum show left audiences nostalgic for a bygone era, though at the price of glossing over painful historical realities, such as the failed Nasserite project of pan-Arabism. Yet the longing for that enchanted world calls upon the audience to connect the dots and fill in the gaps.

CHAPTER FOUR

I Light Ten Candles: Women and Vow-Making[1]

omen in the Arab Middle East, whether they be Muslim or Christian, have traditionally been the conduit of vow-making. In Europe the presenting of vows goes back to early medieval times when the church exercised great power, and at the same time served the feudal system. Simple folk filled the coffers of their feudal overlords, while the church levied huge sums from the simple people, particularly women.

Today women throughout Arab countries still contribute sizable portions of their incomes in order to fulfill vows, by lighting candles, for example, or offering actual sums of money to the church or mosque. Some women also vow to sweep the shrine of some holy man or woman, or volunteer other services to benefit the shrine and its visitors. At every mosque and shrine a collection bin (*sanduq al nuthur*) for vows stands at the entrance; at churches the collection bin may be near the icon of a saint, or at different sites within the church. (Candles are often lit at the four corners of a shrine.)

Vows are usually only delivered when the person has been satisfied that his or her wish has been fulfilled. For instance, a Coptic mother might make a vow to fast for the 55 days of Lent if her son or daughter succeeds in her high school diploma. (Passing the high school diploma is such a critical rite of passage that it can determine what kind of a future a young man or woman will have. It is the passport to upward social mobility, a profession, and a better life all in all. So working-class, as well as middle-class, women place great

importance on such matters.) One might also vow to fast for
the cure of a sick relative, to win a lawsuit, to become fertile,
or to satisfy an important personal need. Women of both
faiths strongly believe that vows to certain saints, or holy
men and women, help solve their problems.

The Coptic calendar is virtually spread with days of fast
year round, in addition to the weekly Wednesday and Friday
when strict practitioners should not eat dairy foods or meats.
Some practice even stricter dietary rules by eating only
boiled vegetables, with salt and other spices the only
additions. The other fasts are Lent (which for Copts extends
to 55 days) and advent (usually three weeks). A special 15-
day fast for the Virgin Mary during the month of August,
the fast of the Apostles, and the fast for Jonah are some of
the most practiced rituals that are often dedicated as vows.

Fasting is an important means of fulfilling vows for
Muslim women, too. In addition to vowing to fast for the
month of Ramadan (which is one of the Pillars of Islam),
women and men may vow to fast extra days. Some Muslims
may vow to fast some of the days prescribed for Copts,
such as the fifteen days for the Virgin Mary. Such crossover
between Muslims and Christians is one of the most
interesting social practices that cement interfaith relations in
countries of the Arab world that have sizable Christian
communities. Muslims and Christians both visit shrines or
sites, especially during the Mawlids (celebration of a saint or
holy man or woman), and churches of revered saints such
Mar Guirguis (Saint George), Mar Mina, and Mar Morcos
(Saint Mark), or the famous church of Saint Theresa in
Shubra, a predominantly Christian suburb of Cairo. Saint
Theresa's church is part of the Catholic diocese highly
revered by all segments of society, rich and poor, Christian
and Muslim. By the same token, Copts are known to
participate in the birthdays of some revered Muslim saints,
such as al-Sayyid al-Badawi in Tanta or Sidi Mursi Abu al-

Abbas in Alexandria. Muslims are also known to visit the many monasteries throughout Egypt seeking the advice and blessings of the monks.

According to research conducted by the sociologist Muhammad Awad Khamis, women mostly make vows for the following reasons: 1) for themselves or their husbands to become fertile, 2) for the relief of physical or mental impairments, 3) for the cure of sick children, 4) for the success of children in school or college, 5) for a successful marriage with a specific person, 6) for the return of a renegade husband, 7) for the marriage of a spinster daughter. These are all positive, well-wishing vows. There are cases, however, when vows are used negatively, to wish evil upon the vow-maker's offenders—a betraying husband, a treacherous woman who has "stolen" her man, a meddling neighbor, and so forth. So vows can take on different forms, though in most cases they are meant for constructive, positive causes.

x.᪣.x

Many are the popular sayings that attest to the importance of such customs. It is common for someone to declare in the course of a conversation that she would vow to light a dozen candles for such and such a saint or holy person, if only he or she would fulfill his or her wish. Here are some typical examples:

Wi hayatik ya sitt ya tahira la 'aaiid dastit shamm' law ha'aatti.

O pure lady I promise to light a dozen candles if you fulfill my wish.

Law rabbini y'bligh al maksud, likki al halawa...

If God fulfills my wish, O holy one I will offer you a gift (money)...

I promise to wash the floors of your shrine with rose water.

May the Lord enable you to do good works, O Imam Shafei',
and I promise to fast ten days in your honor.

If my wish is fulfilled, I promise to pray in your shrine, O
Hussein, my Lord and Martyr, O kinsman of the Prophet,
and his beloved. I promise to fast ten full days from dawn to
dusk.

O holy one... if you help me take revenge on such and such,
I promise to sweep the floors of the mosque, or shrine, make
it shine and sparkle..."

I promise to cook a hearty meal of lentils and beans for the
poor, O pure Lady.

Khamis notes in his research that most of the women who
undertake these vows are poor, although middle- and upper-
class women are known to make similar vows,
commensurate with their social standing and differing levels
of income. A rich woman, for instance, would be more likely
to offer a slaughtered calf than a modest lentil and bean
soup. Christian Coptic women are known to offer to sew the
priest's garments, or to organize church events, and so forth.

The interesting mixture of superstition, religious ritual, and
in some cases pure belief in magic that this practice of vow-
making embodies is still very much with us at the dawn of this
new century. Vow-making is still shrouded in mystery, yet
these practices harken back to ancient Egypt. In a papyrus
known as *Papyrus Magique Comte* we get an interesting
perspective on such practices in the early Christian era in
Egypt of the fourth or fifth century.[2] Here we get a co-
mingling of magic and Christian beseeching for help from
Christ and the Virgin Mary, as well as all the angels and

archangels as Gabriel, Mikhail, Sourial, Zakaria the saint, other martyrs, and regular folk. This particular papyrus, we are told, was written against an individual named Yacub (Jacob) and included the following invocations:

> O Michael O Gabriel O Sourial (all archangels) a meteor will fall from the heavens, and cause leprosy... may the deceased one enter the tomb after he (Yacub) is afflicted with leprosy, may the 5,400 martyrs make him enter his tomb with leprosy.

> O Mary who gave birth to Christ, make him descend in his tomb with leprosy... (and so forth).

We know that in ancient Egypt magical incantations were written on earthenware vessels, papyrus, and linen fabric. In modern day Egypt there are still remnants of these customs. especially among women who seek the help of people who are though to practice magic. These people become all the rage, sometimes even in upper class society, even in Alexandria or Cairo, not just the provinces. It is clear that these magicians exercise great influence over their subjects, and inspire them with awe and reverence. Those so-called magicians are both male and female and share common characteristics. Some dissatisfied subjects who have stopped frequenting the magicians have shed light on their practices, in many cases exposing their quackery.

Most report similar experiences of locale and atmosphere. The spaces these magicians occupy are almost always empty, small rooms without any furniture except for some cushions and pillows. The lights are kept dim, with a coal burner next to the magician sending up the strong aroma of incense and a red glow that mysteriously lights the magician's face. A ceramic vessel filled with water stands near by, and next to it different sizes of paper, cardboard, or small pieces of leather. Dazed women can barely recount what words the magician utters—"Allah, darwish, Satan, heavens, stars, slave"—some combination of words that never seem to become a fully meaningful and comprehended sentence. Witnesses report hearing sudden loud noises, such as heavy breathing, groans, hysterical laughter, or religious incantations of varying rhythms. The magician then calls on Shamhourish or 'Idarous (the devil), asking him what he, the ruling spirit, wants. Then the magician addresses the seeker, asking her to pray for forgiveness from the angels. This might be followed by a sudden cold draft of air, which of course makes the seeker shiver. The magician might then begin a breathtaking avalanche of questions, which the seeker has to answer as quickly as she can. Then the magician responds—perhaps by resuming the muttering of undifferentiated words, perhaps by scribbling on the small pieces of paper. These messages are then folded in leather and thrown into the basin of water. The shadows and special effects play on the imagination. Women have described the leather amulet as floating up to the ceiling. A new voice emerges from the magician, explaining how to use the amulet. Then comes the request for money, in the name of the spirits, and for further visits, perhaps bringing special kinds of fowl, birds, gold jewelry, or some garments or strands of hair from the person in question, upon whose behalf this visitation was made. This is known as *al attr*.

Women from all socioeconomic classes are known to seek the intercession of these magicians, who very often gain influential status and fame, but it is the working class woman who suffers the most, for they have to come up with the designated sums of money as well as the objects required, and very often they are forced to sell their meager possessions to do so. Many a poor woman has given up the jewelry she acquired at her weddings (jewelry actually meant to be part of her dowry, a hedge against hard times). And these women are often the victims of imposters, not unlike the Tarot card readers we see proliferating in Western big cities, or the voodoo priests and priestesses of other cultures.

Another ritual, the *zar*, is still very much practiced by both men and women for different reasons and multiple motivations. It is believed that the word *"zar"* is not of Arabic origin, but rather of an Amharic, Ethiopian source. Samuel Zwemer, in his early study, *The Influence of Animism on Islam*, suggests that *"zar"* came from the verb *"zar,"* meaning "to visit"—the idea being that the *jinn* visit humans. Other scholars opt for the more likely theory that the *zar* came to Egypt via the Sudan, which in turn had received it from Ethiopia, where the ritual of *zar* reigns supreme. *Zar* sessions were regularly held in Mecca, Saudi Arabia in the early 1920s, and were attended by all classes.

In all these countries the *zar* session is meant to alleviate physical and psychological diseases that otherwise do not seem to have any medical cures. These sessions are meant to please the *assyad*, who are not considered demons by any means, for they are neither good nor evil, but pure spirits, who have to be respected. These *assyad* do not inhabit the bodies of humans constantly, but rather visit them on occasion, hence the "sick" subject is not held responsible for his actions, or bodily movements. In fact, it is said instead that the victim is "possessed," or, as they say in Arabic, *maskun*. These *assyad* are held in high esteem—the "syad" part of the word means "master." Indeed, they are believed to be a higher form of existence than human beings.

The *zar* is celebrated ritualistically for certain ailments. Women who seek cures or relief from certain diseases or ailments seek out the *qodia*, who usually demand *al attr*—often a piece of clothing that the *qodia* says she will place under her pillow. Before sleeping, she pledges to recite verses from the *Quran*, so that she may identify in her dreams the source of the disease and what to offer as a remedy and as payment. Of course, the *assyad*'s demands seem to rise with the social and economic stature of the supplicant. Hence she may ask for a modest gift of chicken and cheap silver jewelry from one person, and raise the ante to ask for a camel and gold jewelry from another.

The *qodia* may ask the supplicant to join in preparing the way by melting a cube of sugar in the mouth before going to sleep or drinking rose water, or putting out a loaf of bread sprinkled with salt and sugar so as to gain the approval of the *assyad*. The common denominator in all *zars* is the colored chicken, or red cock. A white-feathered hen for an elderly lady, a black chicken for an Ethiopian maid. The *qodia* invariably sees another animal in the dream—a black goat or a red-headed sheep—and all will be slaughtered at two in the morning, before the *zar*. At sunset before the ceremony, the *kursi* is set. A tray covered with a red cloth is put out upon a round table. Different nuts, dried dates, sugar, and even soap, fill the tray. All manner of fruits, cakes, Turkish delights, sweets, cheeses, dried meats, a bottle of alcoholic beverage and milk are placed out. Huge candlesticks, and many candles, adorn the table. Over this spread, the *qodia* chants all the appropriate verses and songs in honor of the *assyad* (spirits), seeking their approval, while incense burns and the drums are beaten. The "bride," as the "sick" subject is called, is dressed in a new white gown and enters the room with her head held high. Friends would accompany her, dressed in new colorful clothes, happy to participate in the festivities where they move and dance freely. They all believe firmly in the power of the *qodia*, and they seek the blessings and approval of the *assyad*.

Later that night, after the sheep or goat is slaughtered, the face, arms, shoulders, feet and white gown of the subject are covered with blood. Ablutions of the birds take place (the fowl are cleansed with water) and incense is burned; then they, too, are slaughtered, and once more the blood is spread on the subject. The *qodia* gets half of the cleaned, slaughtered animal, in addition to its pelt, feet and head, heart and liver, and as all the bones. The remains are to be buried in a special small room in the house of the *qodia* known as "*al-mayanga*," which is also thought to be the meetingplace for the *assyad*. (The word is "*al-mayanga*" is exclusively Egyptian; it is not found in any other neighboring language or country.)

After removing the bloodstained clothing, the subject dons another set of clean white clothes, a transparent veil, and all her jewelry. The music starts—drums, tambourines, whistles—and the incense burns. The *quodia* sings and compels her subject to cross a burning fire seven times, and then passes incense over the heads of all present (for a special fee). Each of the *assyad* has its own unique tune and rhythm, so for instance *al-jinn al ahmar* (the red demon), or *sitt safina*, or *abu al-khitt*, each elicits a different song. With each tune, the *quodia* changes her clothing, helped along by the women, since she is deep under the spell of the *assyad*.

At the dawn of the 21st century why do such customs as *zar* and vow-making bring comfort to women both educated and illiterate? These old customs proliferate alongside serious attempts to adopt Western solutions such as therapy. Yet many women choose instead to harken back to customs that can be traced, in some cases, to antiquity; perhaps it is a way of establishing connections between the ancient and the modern. We are told that the stories about supernatural beings that are so abundant within Egyptian folklore are not the product of the storyteller's imagination, but rather emanate from a belief system deeply ingrained in Egyptian culture, a belief system not anathema to either Muslims or Christians, but full of *jinn* believed to have inhabited the earth and the heavens, where they eavesdropped on angels and reported back to the diviners on earth who called on them.

Just as in the West interest in the occult sciences never seems to fade, whether it be Tarot card readings, horoscopes, numerology, or the I Ching (it often involves a great curiosity in the customs of both the Near and Far East), women in the Middle East are in a sense reclaiming a heritage that traditionally seemed to answer some of their deep seated anguishing quests.

Yet the stigma attached to seeking psychiatric or psychological help is gradually disappearing amongst all classes of society. It is much more acceptable now for people to talk freely about being depressed, for example, and discussing how to cope with such ailments. Many a time a cab driver might volunteer the information that he was suffering from *ikti'aab nafsi* (depression), and that he is seeking help (or thinking about seeking help). Depression is talked about on radio and television talk show programs by well known experts in the medical and sociological fields. More and more young women talk more openly about sleep disorders as well as eating disorders, and seek professional help. So the traditional and the modern live side by side within these societies in transition.

CHAPTER FIVE

"A New Vision of the Veil," by Iqbal Barraka

*T*his essay is by Iqbal Barraka, the editor-in-chief of the prestigious weekly magazine, Hawa, one of the oldest women's magazines in the Arab world with a readership that can be counted in the millions. Barraka's editorials are known for their uninhibited stances, wit, and learning. Once a student of English literature, she went on to carve a successful career as a journalist who fosters women's issues on all fronts. She has devoted her life to writing about what she has observed, learned, and thought.

This recent piece (translated by M. Mikhail, with Ayten Heykal) is an excerpt from a penetrating, frank, and intimate book that is bound to make waves in the Islamic world. Barraka spent several years researching and working on this book, much of it reading and analyzing the Quran and Hadith (traditions concerning the sayings and doings of the Prophet), as well as other pertinent religious texts and exegesis dealing directly with the role of women.

Simone de Beauvoir once wrote that "feminine literature is in our day animated less by a wish to demand our rights than by an effort toward clarity and understanding." Iqbal Barraka's contribution is certainly this kind of effort, although it may in the process provoke dissent and give rise to controversy in certain circles, since she so clearly believes that women have long been relegated to second place in the world of men. Recognizing that this is more the result of social and educational tradition than any innately "feminine" characteristics, she is here particularly interested in investigating the symbol and role of the hijab (veil).

Ever since the mid-1970s the phenomenon of the veil (*hijab*) began to spread rapidly among Arab women. It created much apprehension among educated Muslim elites. The Western media covered it with much sensation, arousing the curiosity of its uninformed audiences. The ongoing debates among contemporary Muslims on social issues are not, however, limited to the question of the *hijab*. Those who advocate the *hijab* defend their position on the premise that it essentially symbolizes and embodies Islamic identity.

It is a fact that the number of women who wear the veil is on the rise. Preachers in mosques are vehemently encouraging it and the *hijab* has gained wide popularity particularly among the youth who frequent private educational institutions. These young people are the ones who will undoubtedly play a leading role in bringing about change in the future of their country. We witness, too, though, an increase in the popularity of different head coverings—the turban, the *khimar*,[1] the *burkaa*[2]—among young women in Egypt and the Arab world, without any clear-cut religious justification to this fad.

Meanwhile Muslim women are agonizing: Should I wear the *hijab*? Should I not wear the *hijab*? Should I uncover my face and the palms of my hands or hide them? Is it enough to wear a scarf to cover my hair or should I also cover my neck? Is the *niqab*[3] permissible or not? If I do not wear the *hijab* am I a sinner or am I disobedient (as has been mentioned repeatedly in some popular books) or is God all Merciful? If I were to wear the *hijab* will I seem backward, victim to a harem mentality, forfeiting a world of freedoms and rights?

"It is our duty to understand and define the position of Shari'a law regarding the *hijab* and the need to change it." So wrote Qasim Amin, in *The Emancipation of Women*, at the turn of the century. That great reformer and champion of women's rights attacked the *niqab* and the *burqaa* as definitely not decreed by Islam: not for prayer, not as a social norm. He considered them rather as probable cause for *fitna* (sedition). He spoke of the *hijab* as a reason for confining women to their homes and forbidding them from mingling with men. He believed that this custom pertained solely to the wives of the prophet (as has been traditionally understood by all the interpreters of the *Quran* without exception, since they stipulated that believers should study carefully "the reasons surrounding each sura's revelation.")

The Almighty dictates in the *Quran*: "Indeed you are not like other women." The wives of the prophet are not to be likened to the average woman, who was not expected to wear the veil. Qasim Amin urges that women are to be respected no matter whether they wear the veil or not. He believed, in fact, that the veil diminished the status of women and that by forcibly imposing it, serious problems were bound to ensue, which would ultimately create obstacles for women. He redirects us to a verse from the *Quran*: "Allah desires ease for you and desires not hardship for you" (2:185).

Qasim Amin also believed that the donning of the veil could conjure lust precisely because it leaves so much to the imagination. It is evident that women who are unveiled and who protect their honor and chastity and keep their dignity, deserve even greater credit than those who are veiled, for the chastity of the veiled is an imposed condition, while that of the unveiled is voluntary. As he put it, "I do not know how we can boast of the chastity and honor of our women when they are forcefully protected by guards and incarcerated behind secure locks and high walls."

Writing at the end of the nineteenth century, Qasim Amin called not for the immediate or total lifting of the veil, but rather a gradual process of lifting the veil. He believed that doing away with the veil abruptly could lead to dire consequences that would be counterproductive, as is the case with any sudden imposed change. He preferred preparing the minds of young girls for this change so that they would gradually get used to their new independence and believe that honor and dignity are natural, innate qualities.

Qasim Amin also believed that young women should be allowed to interact with male relatives and strangers, within the limits of religious dictates and social ethics under the guidance of their parents. This would naturally make it easier for these young women to deal in public life with men without, as he put it, "any danger of sedition wherever they may live in urban, rural or desert locales." He reiterated these positions as well in his second book, *The New Woman*, in which he predicts the gradual disappearance of the veil and its eventual demise. In answer to those who claim that the *hijab* was decreed in the Holy Book, he replies:

> Religious laws are truthful and just and timeless and conform to ethical norms and good habits. These religious laws were relegated to people who applied their best knowledge and effort to explain them. This is what happened after the death of the prophet Muhammad and his followers. The basic rules or commandments are not subject to change or replacement, but religious laws pertinent to customs are subject to change according to place and time. For example ,uncovering the head was traditionally considered improper and lacking dignity by Easterners, while Westerners do not share these views. These customs clearly have no relation to religion but rather are inherited customs. If we comply with all that our forefathers dictated we face the sure danger of weakening the Islamic nation, petrifying the mind, chaining the feet and shackling the hands. This would ultimately result in preventing the Islamic nation from protecting its well-being and defending her right to exist, advancing toward happiness and moreover causing its utter demise (page 114).

Qasim Amin wrote his seminal work *The Emancipation of Women* at the end of the 19th century, at a time when women were confined in their homes and denied all human rights. Their only outlet to the world was through their latticed windows. Amin made it his lifelong goal to write in defense of women. He places the discussion of the veil within the larger framework of the woman question, and in so doing defends her well-being and right to a better life. He pleaded with men to liberate women; he suggested founding an organization for fathers who wished to rear their daughters in this manner. Qasim Amin was indeed the right person to clamor for the liberation of women: "The time has come for the elders, the wise men of the nation and the government, the thinkers and writers to direct their attention to the condition of the Egyptian women. I do not find a more pressing question and one worthier of their attention than this one."

Even after his book was received with great opposition, he never gave in, but followed up with another book in 1901, heralding the beginning of the twentieth century, and defending the liberators of women with equal fervor. He wrote the following about the veil:

> Forcing women to wear the *hijab* is one of the cruelest and worst forms of enslavement because men in the age barbarism enslaved women, they captured, bought and sold them and in all cases believed they owned them totally. Man deprived women of their human dimension, limiting them to one function only—his personal, physical pleasures. He confined her to his place of residence, refused to let her leave it without his permission and prohibited any other person from enjoying her company either by looking at her or speaking with her, as if she were an object to be enjoyed and exploited exclusively by her owner. Since it became increasingly impossible to confine women in their place of residence, he sought to have her wear the *hijab* and never show her face, especially in public. Initially imposed on the wife, the *hijab* was gradually enforced on the daughters, sisters and mothers, all womenfolk. The *hijab* is the definition of this old form of ownership and the remnant of past barbaric customs which dominated generations.

All this was before the realization that human beings are not objects to be possessed because they happen to be female or black and subject to be enslaved by the white man. In another instance he quotes an Indian thinker, Amin Aly al-

Qadi, whose work was translated in the *Muqtataf* magazine, in the two issues published in June and July of 1899. "One should question whether the wives of the Caliphs (successors of the prophet) and other women appeared totally shrouded, as women today seem to be." Amin believed that women wore a *niqab* to cover their faces, just as women cover their gray hair to appear younger: in other words, there are always considerations of fashion. In India, the burka was not even known at this time, and there the women of the upper classes would appear without veils. Qasim Amin pointedly states that in the reign of Mu'aiwiwya, Arabs practiced castration, a custom borrowed from the Byzantines, and in the reign of the second Ummayad dynasty, al-Mutawaqil (sometimes called the Nero of the Arabs) emulated the harem system and decreed the separation of women from men in public celebrations. But up until the end of the sixth century of the Hegira (which is the eighth CE, for the Muslim calendar counts from 622, Mohammad's emigration from Mecca to Medina), women mingled openly with men. They were known to meet with guests and join in great celebrations and festivities. Women partook in warfare wearing shields and helped their men folk defend their homes and fortresses. In the middle of the seventh century (of the Hegira), when the Arab empire began to disintegrate under the onslaught of the Tatars, religious jurists began debating the validity of women showing their hands and feet in public.

Khalil Abd al-Karim, a religious jurist, born in Aswan, Egypt and imprisoned between 1954–65 as a Muslim brother, writes about misinterpreted concepts attributed to Islam:

> The custom of segregating women began in the early conquest of Muslims of Persian lands when the Abbasids intermingled with the Persians. Out of fear, they imposed the *hijab* on women. For instance, as far as Muslim dress today is concerned, there is no text that decrees that the color white is not to be worn by anyone but the Prophet. Women can wear it at the mosque and on other occasions or at funerals.

Khalil Abd al-Karim categorically states that there are no restrictions prohibiting Muslims from wearing whatever they wish. In the books of tradition, the Prophet himself is known to have worn a variety of outfits, as well as clothes of many colors. He is believed to have worn every kind of headdress fashionable in his time—the turban, the *kalansowa* (a headdress similar to what is worn today by Eastern Orthodox clergy), a helmet, to name a few. There is no evidence, however, that he wore the skullcap widely worn by Muslims today of all religious sects. At the time of the revelation of the *Quran*, clothing was a sign of wealth and social status and hence a way to show off, as it has always been in Semitic groups. That is why the Prophet warned, "On the Day of Judgment, God will not look kindly upon he who is boastful."[4]

There is no objection, however, to paying attention to one's apparel. God Almighty permits the wearing of good clothing. Khalil Abd al-Karim objects to the return of the *niqab* as there is no evidence of its being decreed in either the *Quran* or the Hadith. He narrates an incident about a female follower who was wearing the *niqab*, who came to the Prophet and cried out, "Fire! Fire!" He asked, " What is your complaint, oh, servant of God?" He admonished her to unveil her face.

Some Muslim women in history are known not to have covered their faces, among them Aisha, Bint Talha, and Asma, daughter of Abu Bakr, as well as nieces of Aisha. Khalil Abd al-Karim explains in his *Wrong Interpretations Attributed to Islam* that if the reasons justifying the *hijab* are presumably to comply with the verses of the *Quran*, then an attempt must be made to put them within their rightful context, to know to whom these verses were addressed and the surrounding occasion of their revelation. Why is it, he asks, that fundamentalists use modern medical drugs instead of traditional remedies such as oils, balsams, and henna, et cetera, although they are clearly mentioned in religious texts? The well-being of a society is no less important than the well-being of individuals. Finally he adds,

> It is evident that every generation faces new conditions and in the future will inevitably have to grapple with new experiences, since the impetus of life is change. Looking backward and yearning for the past only freezes the mind and is not to the advantage of Shari'a law or beneficial to its followers. What is to be done when Islamists are blindly following and applying uncritically dictates not using their minds in spite of the fact that Islam has given great importance to approach matters rationally.

Another staunch opponent of *hijab* is the former chief justice of the Egyptian Court of Appeals Mohammed Said al-Ashmawi, who published an important book a number of years ago, *The Truth about the Hijab and Evidence in Support of Hadiths* in the respected series al Kitab al Dhahabiyy (Rose el Yusuf, 2002). The author, a well known thinker and writer whose works in Shari'a law and *fiqh* (jurisprudence) are taught at major foreign universities in the West, categorically refutes the misinterpretations of the Quranic dictates. He believes that the course followed by extremists leads precisely to a misrepresentation of the *Quran*. The greatest difficulties faced by a serious scholar are opinions of inflexible positions. Ashmawi considers apparel to be part of customs and traditions, with no connection to religion or Shari'a law, except to the extent that it is required to be decent, dignified, and clean. He also believes that the *hijab* in its current use is a political symbol, enforced by religious groups to prove the extent of their influence but by no means a religious dictate decreed in the holy *Quran* or the Prophet's traditions. He also warns against those who claim that the *hijab* is decreed by consensus. By reiterating that the *hijab* is decreed in the *Quran*, extremists accuse those who oppose them of heresy and apostasy. (Those who clamor for the return of the *hijab* base themselves on verse 31 al-Nur and verse 60 Ahzab.[5]) If applying Islamic jurisprudence is by definition necessary in this situation, if there is a verdict, then it follows there must be proof and fact, and if there is no proof, the verdict must be lifted. The basis of the verdict mentioned in the verse that distinguishes between free women and slaves is not valid anymore, since slavery has long been abolished. Only the Prophet's women were banned from leaving their homes except when responding to the call of nature, and had to be protected from being accosted by strangers. Since that rule is nonexistent now, its application should be null and void.

Khalid ibn Doreh, a collector of Hadiths, cites one about Aisha, one of the Prophet's wives, in which the Prophet is quoted as saying, "If a woman reaches puberty, she should show only the face and hands. Said al-Ashmawi contends that this Hadith contradicts another one attributed to Aisha, which says that the Prophet said that a woman is not allowed to show any part of her body except her face, hands, and forearms. Both Hadiths are based on individuals' hearsay and not considered a matter of consensus or widely recognized, and the difference between the two is substantial. One deals with what is more appropriate under certain societal conditions. The other is written with theological concerns of what is permissible and what is not permissible. Some of the jurists believe that whatever emanated from the Prophet, even laws, were temporary and relevant to specific problems of contemporary conditions, so if conditions change, as, for example, the Hadith when the Prophet says, "Shave your mustaches and grow your beards as a means of distinguishing between believers and non-believers." Ashmawi wonders what it really means to have a consensus of jurists. Does it mean a consensus among the Prophet's companions, as Ibn Hanbal believed? Wahabis adhere to this, since they object to the principle of consensus as a rule. Or a consensus among the people of Medina? Or Kufa, or Basra? A consensus of Sunnis or Shi'ites, or both? Where does it end?

CHAPTER SIX

Women in the Discourse of Crisis, by Nasr Hamid Abu-Zeid

Nasr Abu-Zeid, professor in the Department of Arabic Literature at Cairo University, was catapulted onto the international scene when a group of Islamist lawyers launched a lawsuit claiming that since Abu-Zeid's writings prove him an "apostate," (according to them) he must divorce his wife, for he is unfit to be married to a Muslim woman. In August of 1996, the highest court of appeals upheld this ruling, and since then the couple has been living in the Netherlands in self-imposed exile, awaiting still further rulings.

The grounds upon which the case against Abu-Zeid has been built are his writing, which argue that religious texts should be interpreted in their original context. He further argues that other economic and sociological interpretive frameworks should be used to better comprehend these texts. As he puts it, "Since language develops with the development of society and culture, providing new ideas and developing its terminology to express more developed relations, then it is only natural to re-interpret texts in their original historical and social context, replacing them with more contemporary interpretations that are humanistic and developed, while keeping the content of the verses stable."

In his writings, Abu-Zeid addresses a variety of issues pivotal to Islamic thought. He re-assesses the appropriate role of religion in contemporary life. His work al-Mar'a fi khitab al-azma (Women in the Discourse of Crisis) is a brilliant revisiting of the Nahda (Arab Renaissance) discourse and its centrality to the woman question.[1] He lucidly deconstructs the concept of sectarianism and logically shows the intimate relationship *between the so-called "fitna ta'ifiyya" (religious strife and the woman question.) He examines the spreading of sectarian strife, in places such as Bosnia and Herzegovina, and the virulent attacks on the Muslim population within Europe, elucidating the historical contexts that sanctions such atrocities.*

This work addresses the systematic attack mounted on the Nahda discourse. In an introduction and four chapters he travels widely, from the anthropological aspects of language, to the wounded identity, to Tunisian legislative discourse. In the chapter called "The Sectarian and the Nahda Discourse," which I have here translated, Abu-Zeid systematically analyzes the arguments of the contemporary Islamic discourse and their position vis-à-vis the Nahda national unity and the woman question. He offers a re-reading of Qasim Amin, as well as the Tunisian thinker al-Tahir al-Haddad. He shows how the new way of thinking spawned by the Nahda discourse early in the century is in serious danger of being smothered by the climate of anti-intellectualism and religious militancy.

x⟐x

We can assess the woman question from several angles, especially when we view, on the one hand, the complexity of the contemporary societal structure and, on the other, the intertwining relations in societies in the modern era. Indeed, the woman question has numerous dimensions within social, cultural, and intellectual spheres. Added to this complexity and interrelationship is the religion so central to our Arab and Muslim societies. It continues to represent a legal and legitimate reference point as well as a spiritual and moral point of reference.

There is no doubt that renewing the discussion of the woman question in the Arab and Islamic world cannot be divorced from the phenomenon some call "Islamic revival" and others call "Islamic Fundamentalism." No matter what the nomenclature of this phenomenon, be it positive or negative, its reality is central and pivotal in raising many questions that we all thought were once and for all resolved within the Nahda discourse, especially when dealing with the woman question.

Here is it essential to reiterate what is already well known, namely that the crisis of Arab and Islamic existence that reached its peak with the June 1967 defeat constitutes the beginning of the unraveling of all that was once believed to be constant and immutable. Thus began a trend of questioning on all fronts and on every level which continues to this day, and we do not think that it is about to end. Perhaps, we postulate, the after-shocks of the seismic event of the defeat continue in such a way as to keep the mind, as it were, in a perpetual state of breathlessness, rendering it incapable of assessing problems, let alone solving them. No sooner had the Arabs absorbed the defeat and devised methods for dealing with it (by October 1973), than they discovered that additional defeats were in store for them. Thus the invasion of Beirut, the invasion of Southern Lebanon, the 1991 Gulf War, an imposed peace, and so forth, ensued in succession. These political setbacks gave rise to narrow ethnic, sectarian strife, sometimes taking on regional dimensions. That strife tended to imprison the "individual," be it man or woman, within strict boundaries of allegiances where the "other" was to be more or less excluded.

If we proceed beyond the Arab situation, it will be clear that the political break-up of the Soviet Union constitutes a "defeat" within the larger human spectrum. This defeat has, in turn, led to almost similar results on the world scene. By that, I mean the dominance of the ethnic and sectarian trends, not only within what has come to be known as totalitarian societies, but within all European societies. The phenomenon took on the shape of bloody sectarian wars in Yugoslavia; in Czechoslovakia the break-up was more peaceful. Yet the dominance of the sectarian mentality was not limited to these two societies.

If we transcend the concept of the economic and political unity of the European Common Market project with its cultural and intellectual dimensions, we shall discover that this European unity has built into it a "fencing-in" dimension, that is, a barrier has been erected between European and non-European countries. This is clearly seen in the explosive areas around the world where double standards are clearly applied, such as, for instance, the direct American/European intervention in the Middle East in quest of international legitimacy, in return for a retreat vis-à-vis the wars of ethnic cleansing and extermination against the Muslims in Bosnia and Herzegovina. Also, one can mention the very impulsive interference in Somalia and the total silence toward the repressive policies of Israel against the Palestinians.

This larger world condition partakes in fueling additional ethnic sectarianism in the Arab world which, when it does not find a breather in interfacing with the real enemy (backwardness, dictatorship, and imperial hegemony), backfires on itself. Have the barbaric attacks on thousands of Muslim women in Bosnia and Herzegovina (which went as far as inseminating some of them with animal semen in laboratory experiments) had any impact on the Arab and Islamic world except the pouring of more fuel on the fires of wrath that enflame the Islamic discourse, not only against Europe and Europeans, but against a culture and civilization that sanctions such attacks? In other words, we must say that if the Islamic discourse has become impermeable in its fundamentalism as a result of these defeats, then the conditions in the world have contributed to deepening that mentality of entrenchment within fundamentalism.

We shall not here refer to what has been known as an American and European tendency to make Islam an ideological enemy, in whose opposition is harnessed the power and solidarity of the West, which, in turn, protects its economic interests in the lands of the Muslims in general and in those of the Arabs in particular. This phenomenon is linked to the US and Europe's capacity for utilizing the ruling Islamic political powers to their own ends. This continuing dominance and hegemony leads to fragmentation, fueling the fires of conflict within Arab societies to the extent, perhaps, of bringing them to the brink of civil warfare on an intellectual, if not physical, level.

Sectarianism: The Break-Up of the Individual

Sectarianism is a divisionary act, a breaking up that does not cease at a defined point. It may start at a given point, but if it is not contained very quickly, it simply explodes, just as fascist and Nazi Europe would have destroyed everything in its path had it not been for the general resistance during World War II. We cannot quite determine that first breaking point in our Arab world. Did it emanate from within or from without? In fact, the breaking points and the meeting points are numerous. The important thing to remember is that this sectarianism began early with the crisis of the 1967 defeat. Note that the events of Black September and the massacres following it closely within a few years of the defeat continued to shatter all structures and systems, culminating in the fragmentation of the individual. And just as the breaking up of an atom, when the electron is fissured from the nucleus, creates a frightening source of energy, so does sectarianism break the human being in half, into male and female, into a relationship in which the male rules over the female totally and absolutely. Something similar to that happened immediately after the defeat, and this grew exponentially to the point where the human being as an individual was shattered to pieces.

In the beginning, the destroyed group reached out for its

roots, to its "heritage" which, to some, represented a protection from the nakedness of defeat. For others, it was an opportunity to question, to research, to study, to contemplate, to meditate. As the momentum of the sectarian break-up grew, each current barricaded itself within a closed discourse that refused to recognize the discourse of the other, or to enter into any form of immediate or direct dialogue with it. Hence we can say that, with some necessary simplification, there were two intellectual trends: Islamic fundamentalism (with all its different currents and trends) and secular humanism (with all its gradations and nuances).

In short, the fundamentalist way of thinking, with which we are particularly concerned, continued to launch its attacks against its sworn enemy. Its aim was to distort the external cultural and intellectual frameworks belonging to this "enemy." This is what, for instance, took place in Said Qutb's discourse in Egypt, a discourse emanating from that of another fundamentalist thinker, Abdula'la al-Mawdudi. The latter is considered one of the fruits of sectarianism, one that was planted by British colonialism in the Indian subcontinent between Muslims and Hindus, a sectarianism that cost Gandhi, the Indian freedom fighter, his life.

Said Qutb did not preoccupy himself much with the cause of women, except for the "sexual" side of things (against the "nudity" and "mixing" that European society presumably allowed between the sexes). His criticism was primarily addressed to the European way of life which, according to him, experienced "contradictions in the realm of thought" between religion and everyday living. Thus the European way of life was far removed from the system of "god," having submitted instead to the system of "mankind." Hence his criticism of Freud or Freudianism, which he simply placed within the category of "sexual degradation." His criticism of Darwinian thought was particularly severe, categorizing it as "animalism," an animalism upon which the sexual

interpretation of human behavior was based. His critique of
Marxism was equally virulent.

The critique of Europe in the discourse of Qutb was, in one
of its most important aspects, a critique of the Arab and
Egyptian secular discourse, which is, in its very essence, rooted
in European sources. This is the first instance of
fundamentalism's attempt to negate its opposite. The second
aspect of its critique involves the Arab Nahda (Renaissance)
discourse. What is meant here by the Nahda discourse is that
continuous trend starting with Rifa'a al-Tahtawi's *Takhliss al
Ibriz* (Manners and Customs of Modern Parisians) all the way
up to Zaki Naguib Mahmoud's discourse based on rationality.

This critique of the secular heritage was conducted by the
followers of Said Qutb, beginning with Saleh Sirriya (of the
group known as *al-Takfir wal Hijra*) and up to Shaykh Omar
Abdul Rahman and his followers. This critique adopts the
teachings of Said Qutb on the *hakimiyya* (sovereignty) and
jahiliyya (paganism) of systems throughout the world that rely
upon the *hakimiyya* of human beings instead of the *hakimiyya*
of God. Hence there is no hesitation in branding with
apostasy and heresy all those connected with the Nahda
discourse, from Taha Hussein to Salama Mussa to Ali Abdul
Raziq. When the General Egyptian Book Organization
reprinted the collection of books dealing with *tanwir*
(enlightenment) at nominal prices, in an effort to confront the
fundamentalists, they answered with the following question:

> If you truly desire *tanwir*, why have you not published
> alongside these publications the collection of responses these
> works provoked? Why have you not published, for instance,
> the response of the martyr Said Qutb to Taha Hussein's book
> *The Future of Culture in Egypt*?

They proceeded to comment on publication project by stating
that its organizers wished "to revive a flame that is almost
extinct. They want to pour fuel on a fire so that it may burn the
beliefs of Muslims, but God alone will fulfill His goals." That

same writer proceeded to include in that chain of apostasy Taha Hussein, who in turn relays the torch to Amin al-Kholy, who in turn hands it to Mohammed Ahmad Khalafallah— and, finally, to him who is known as Nasr Abu Zeid.[2]

This discourse is its essence appropriates the historical legacy from its opponent. In addition, it has distorted the supposed European roots of the discourse of Nahda. This action of robbing or appropriating is part and parcel of the external and internal sectarian fragmentation. It began by producing a sectarian discourse opposed to the secular discourse that believes in the principle that "religion is for God, and the nation is for all," a slogan that was upheld during the social and political struggle against colonialism and feudalism that came to the forefront during the 1919 Revolution. Hence the problem of religious minorities or religious strife, which led to the phenomenon of sectarian *fitna* (rift/strife) in Egypt since the beginning of the 1980s. This sectarian discourse against the Christian minorities ran parallel to the discourse against women, demanding that women return to the *hijab* (veil) and to the home and asked women to surrender all the gains they may have achieved, with the exception of what they may have attained in the realm of education and limiting that to certain areas which would be appropriate to their femininity.[3] Hence, the schism on the level of society moved to the level of the individual. Here it was that the human being was broken into two halves, a male half and a female half, with the only possible relationship between them limited to the act of procreation and the protection of the species, with the aim of creating a society that is to be ruled by God and not by man.

The Nahda Discourse: Resisting the Break-Up

When the principle "religion is for God, and the nation is for all" began to take shape, it was meant to protect society from the threat of sectarianism from the outside. This began when

Muslims and Christians rallied together refusing all that British colonialism upheld in Egyptian society that was supposed "to protect minorities," but was really the same colonialism that had promoted sectarian strife in the Indian subcontinent. It was no mere coincidence that the events that led to the 1919 revolution were the selfsame ones that saw the beginnings of the unveiling of women following women's active participation in the anti-colonial struggle, the struggle against the British. Qasim Amin's plea for the emancipation of women had had its impact, in spite of the attacks leveled against him and his book by conservatives and those opposing change.

This intimate relation between "national unity" and "women's emancipation," a connection involving the sectarian dimension of the woman question within the contemporary Islamic discourse as well as the attacks on the Nahda discourse and the attempts to denigrate it on every level, found within the discourse on women a golden opportunity to defy and calumniate it. We should not forget that the roots that fuel the dual attacks mentioned above are the same as those we find in the actual conditions of defeat and crisis, even though the question appears to be on the surface a question of struggles between two different discourses, each trying to extricate itself from a situation of crisis.

The difference between the Nahda discourse and the contemporary Islamic discourse is the difference between an attempt at unifying and an attempt at breaking up. It is a difference between the concept of "nation," which depends on the unity of the land, of history, and common interests and the concept or definition of religion, which depends on the unity of belief. So much, then, on the national and local level. As for the relationship with the European "other," the Nahda discourse is an open one that is able to see the other in his progress and economic ambitions. That is why it learns from European tradition so that it can fight it with the same weapons. The Islamic discourse takes an inimical stance toward Europe—a total and unequivocal inimical stance—although this enmity does not stop its political representatives from importing technology and investing huge sums of money in the banks of the West. Conversely, this discourse takes refuge in the heritage that has become the cloak of identity and a specificity that signifies distinction. The position of the Nahda discourse vis-à-vis the heritage is one of mediation, questioning, investigation, and a refusal to compromise with it or with any of its currents and tendencies, having taken account of its plurality and historicity.

We can easily see these differences in the discourse of the Nahda with reference to the question of women where we see that this discourse is, at all times, pulled in two different directions. The first dimension is the weight of development as shown in the direct interaction with the advanced European societies, be it through recognizing their accomplishments in their natural habitat and familiarizing itself with the customs and manners of their people, or coming into contact with them within the different regimes of the Arab nation. The other dimension is namely the interfacing with the West, on the basis that it is a reality we have to deal with rather than one that we would ignore or from which we would attempt to escape. It is a reality that has both its positive and negative sides. As for the negative aspects, we have to face them and deal with them, but not at the expense of the positive aspects. By distinguishing between positive and negative, with reference to the condition of women from the point of view of unveiling and mixing with men, Qasim Amin almost repeats the thesis of Rifa'a al-Tahtawi concerning Parisian women, in which Tahtawi clearly expressed his admiration for their openness and boldness, their vitality and agility of movement. This was not condemned, even if it meant coming in close contact with or touching men when they danced. As Qasim Amin writes in his *Emancipation of Women*,

Events have knocked at our doors. And we have introduced a new manner of intermingling with different nations of the West. There have been created new relations between us and them, contacts which have made us face up to the reality that they are strong and more advanced than we are. And this has led the larger part of our society to imitate them in their customs and manners, particularly if this happened to coincide with gratifying certain lusts or as a means of breaking away from restrictions. This has also led many of our upper classes to be more permissive as regards their wives and their women folk. They showed permissiveness when they let them frequent places of entertainment and allowed them to go to the theater and the like. Many have followed in their footsteps. Of course, some moral-corruption ensued as a consequence. This happened for reasons mentioned above. However, it is not in our interest nor is it acceptable to turn back the clock and resort to "thickening" the veil or the *hijab*. It has, on the contrary, become an important part of our duty to protect these gains and avoid all the negative aspects that resulted there from. This is what is within our capacity to do (84).

Thus we see that the Nahda discourse was well aware of the laws of human behavior as stipulated by Ibn Khaldun. The first and cardinal principle is to focus on where the interest lies and to attempt to reach it. The second principle is the fact that the defeated always mimics the conqueror in his manners, his clothes, and his demeanor. This is what happened in Arab societies when they emulated the West, particularly when it came to satisfying their lusts or breaking away from certain fetters. The third principle, which is the most important for our purposes, is that change may come along with certain corruptions, but these corrupting elements should not lead us to resist change, or to stand against it, so as not to deprive our societies of its positive aspects.

We notice here that this third principle within the discourse of al-Nahda opposes an important principle of the old religious discourse as well as the new religious discourse. This principle, which has been articulated by certain *fuqaha* (scholars or jurists), stipulates that certain "corruptions" that may have some beneficial aspects should be discarded. This position opposes the discourse of the Nahda, which believes in curing the corruption and facing it squarely—a preferred solution to one that would stop the winds of change with all that this may carry for fulfilling one's interests, the interest of individuals as well as the interests of the group and for the welfare of humanity at large. The solution offered by the discourse of the Nahda in general as a cure to the side effects of development (namely corruption) is education that protects women, and even men, from the consequences of such development (Amin 31). Through the discussion of this last mentioned principle, the Nahda discourse addresses the second dimension with which it is interrelated—namely, the dimension of "religion," traditions, and heritage.

It was not possible for the Nahda discourse to discuss the whole question of the legitimacy of the *shari'a* or legal laws, especially since its structure was based on the principle of non-confrontation between itself and development. One of the most important theses of the discourse of the Nahda, as represented in the discourse of Mohammed Abdu, who is considered the prime teacher of Qasim Amin, is that Islam is the religion of freedom, civilization, and progress. The contradictions between the advancement represented by Europe and Islam are based on an ignorance of true Islamic teachings and old and decrepit traditions that have wrongly been attached to Islam. Hence Qasim Amin adhered to the notion that the decline and backwardness of women in Arab and Islamic societies with all the consequences that it entailed of restrictions and the forcing of the veil on women was not to be found in the interpretation of Islam. Its only explanation is the backwardness of these societies, a backwardness that is alien to the teachings and principles of Islam. Qasim Amin believes that the split between Islam and these principles is to be attributed to ignorance and backwardness. This is a condition that could result in a misunderstanding of Islam. Backwardness has many causes within Islamic societies and in their history, which Qasim Amin summarizes as oppression and dictatorship, repeating what Afghani Abdu and Adbul Rahman al-Kawakibi had said earlier (Amin 27).

The nation is moved by different principles, either to leap toward modernity and development or to regress to backwardness and barbarism. These conditions themselves can affect religion and its interpretation. In this close relationship between customs and traditions in every nation, and their position vis-à-vis knowledge and modernity, custom and tradition always take the upper hand and exercise a much strong pull. Custom and tradition are always the furthest away from change. A nation has no other alternative but to respond to this call unless the spirit of the nation changes, rising above or falling below a certain level of its own rationality. Hence we see that custom always overcomes other factors or influences—even the laws. And what we see happening every day in our country reinforces what we have noted. New laws and edicts that are set to better the condition of the nation are changed into new legal instruments that perpetuate corruption. That is no surprise, for customs can have the upper hand over religion itself and can interpret and dilute its interpretation to the extent that people familiar with it would still deny it (Amin 24).

In this sense Islam is acquitted, especially of the deterioration of the condition of women. But this acquittal prepares the way for the discourse of the Nahda to render a new reading of Islam and its texts that opposes the fundamentalists' *salafi* (traditionalist) reading. It underscores what Islam has offered women as regards rights that, in some aspects, go beyond the gains European women achieved after the European Renaissance.

But alas!—foul morals have overtaken a beautiful religion. The morals were inherited from nations where Islam had taken root; each place brought to Islam its own own traditions, myths, and delusions (here is a direct reference to the Turks). Learning and knowledge had not developed in these nations to the same level at which *shari'a* had elevated women. The most important reinforcing of the old customs and traditions was, of course, the tyrannical governments that continue to succeed one another today (Amin 26–27).

This interaction between the European other, representing modernity and advancement, and religion is what granted a certain vitality to the Nahda discourse. This attempt at finding a compromise between two dimensions, independently of the positive aspects and their results, is what gives the discourse of the Nahda its synthesizing characteristic. It steers it away from sectarianism— sectarianism whose axis revolves around the self and which sings its virtues and distinguishes its essence from the "other." This interpretive discourse pulls together, unifies, and attempts to bridge the spaces, unlike the sectarian discourse that aims at fragmentation.

When it comes to the woman question, the Nahda discourse attempts to integrate human beings—be they men or women—in a unified, homogeneous whole. Some may say that what propelled the discourse of the Nahda was a utilitarian principle that sought to energize the productive capacity of society by recruiting women in its ranks.[4] It may be said that the Nahda discourse meant to achieve a compromise (*tawfiq*) but ended up by botching things up (*talfiq*).[5] All of this could be true if looked at critically. But it is also true that the integrative discourse had very serious and important results when it came to the question of women in particular. These results and consequences remained latent, seeds that did not find the right kind of soil to nurture their growth. The discourse of Qasim Amin stood on the borders of "acquitting" Islam of the charge of criminalizing women, but al-Tahir al-Haddad went beyond the logic of defending and acquitting to offering a semi-historical interpretation of the religious texts with reference to women.

Al-Tahir Al-Haddad: Transcending Duality

Since rational *ta'wil* (interpretation) founded by Mohammad Abdu is the point of departure for the reformists to understand Islam, it must be said that *ta'wil* revolves around the attempt to render Islam amenable to the values of modernity, civilization, and progress. Hence we can see how Qasim Amin, following in the footsteps of his teacher Mohammad Abdu, found it necessary to incorporate the principles of learning and modernity in understanding modernity:

> Religious sciences and *fiqh* cannot be rendered useful if they are not preceded by knowledge and scientific principles. Is not *tawhid* the seal of all sciences and the essence of the sum of the whole? Is not *fiqh* the science of *Shari'a*, the science of every spirit in its connection with its creator and in its relationship with the rest of humanity? Both are in need of the knowledge of the science of psychology and both need the science of anatomy, physics, mathematics, biology, and other sciences, all of which help to enhance the mind and human thought. Is not truth one which resembles a tree with different branches, each connected with the other, all feeding from the same root, one root, and all serving one life and producing a fruit which is the true knowledge of everything in the universe (Amin 101)?

The vision of the unity of knowledge, in spite of its multifacetedness and its many branches and roots all finding root in the human mind, rendered religious science a part of human knowledge. In other words, Amin suggested that religious thought should have to submit to the same methodology and approach in terms of understanding, explanation, and analysis. And here, once more, the discourse of the Nahda shows itself again to be a discourse that unifies rather than a discourse that divides, while the opposing fundamentalist *salafi* discourse adopts a methodology that distinguishes between religious sciences and worldly sciences based on the fact that the first takes its root from "belief" whereas the other takes its root from the "mind."[6] This differentiation between the realms of knowledge is in keeping with the fact that the *salafi* discourse is a sectarian discourse from an intellectual and rational point of view. Once more time, we face the social dimension of knowledge and the question of "oppression" and "dictatorship" as forms of corrupt rule responsible for "ignorance" and "backwardness" and the deteriorating condition of women. More important than all this is the responsibility of the latter for the deterioration of religious values. Qasim Amin adds:

> We need not delve into greater detail in explaining something that is known to all and that is the deterioration of religion today—in all its aspects, even in the aspects of worship. We wanted to show that the deterioration of religion follows the deterioration of the mind. The source of all other ills that have stood between us and progress is primarily the failure to educate men and women alike (12).

This explanation, which begins with society as an integrated system and not merely a collection of parts, represents—despite its unsophisticated interpretation—a principle upon which the notion of the unity of knowledge rests. That necessitates that religious knowledge be based on logic in the same manner that other branches of knowledge are based upon it.

If these concepts are scattered throughout the discourse of the Nahda in such a manner that it becomes difficult to reconstitute them as a unified whole, we note that the discourse of al-Tahir al-Haddad concerning women (in 1929, 30 years after Qasim Amin) succeeds in going beyond *al-ta'wil al-Mudad* (alternate reading) of Islam and its texts. He proposes the concepts of "relativity" and "historicity" in his interpretation of the dictates of Islam concerning women. Haddad sees that these were never final decisions but were dictates that rose from the conditions of the society in which Islam appeared, a society in which the condition of women was more akin to slavery than to any other condition. Thus al-Haddad states in his *Women in Shar'ia Law and Society*: "In reality Islam did not give us a final decision as to what is the essence of women."[7] This decision cannot be applicable to all time and in all different phases of development. Islam does not have in its text anything that definitively relegates women to the role they still play in many societies. What we find in Islam, however, in light of the weakness of women and their backwardness in society, is clear evidence of this reality. Hence, the appointment of men as guardians of women and other rulings were built upon this reality. The *fuqaha*, for instance, interpreted questions of inheritance; women inherited half as much as men as a direct consequence of men's role as guardians. Nothing will have us believe that this should be the case forever without any possibility of change, for we find that Islam itself has gone beyond the conditions in which it arose, always expecting to change as time went by. So, for instance, Islam declared that women might enjoy civic freedom when it came to gainful employment and growth of fortune through commerce and trade and the like. Islam granted women security through Wasf al-Dhimma (the guarantee of obligation and protection) so they could deal with and be dealt with within areas where they may not have had prior experience. Note that during that era there were no indications as to its possible success (al-Haddad 31).

With the change in social conditions and the betterment of the condition of women in society, we can read the religious text in its historical context with the intention of getting to its essence and finding the immutable, unchangeable dictates hidden behind the temporal and the changing. A literal reading alone is what stands against such an understanding because it is a reading that negates the societal contexts of the revealing of the *Quran* and its rulings. Thus, al-Tahir al-Haddad refers to the dictates of the *fuqaha* as the "limitations" of the texts and "non-limitations" of reality. But al-Haddad does not linger as the *fuqaha* did on the borders of *qiyas*[8] in its *fiqh* meaning—that is, forcing the new realities onto the teachings, on the pretext of debate or of deducing rulings, as is known in the science of the fundamentals of *fiqh*. Al-Haddad contemplates the phenomenon of *naskh* in the religious text—that is, the changing of *ahkam* (rulings)—and interprets them in their real context given the seriousness of their content.

> Life is long, and the longer it is, the more changes are needed to express its essence and specificity. About 20 years into the life of the Prophet (Peace be upon him) after his founding of Islam, there was a need to abrogate texts by introducing other texts and to replacing rulings with other rulings in keeping with this everlasting *sunna*. So how can continuing generations and centuries unroll in the face of an eternal Islam, while we do not change or alter ourselves (12)?

This life cannot possibly be encompassed by the texts because life is so long; it changes and differs so much more than these texts themselves, which carry within them the imprint of their time and point directly to reality, to the social reality within which they appeared. And hence we have to differentiate between what is "essential" and what is "transient," between what is "constant" and what is "changeable" in our understanding of these texts. Once more, al-Haddad does not stop at "intentions" as defined by the *fuqaha* and fundamentalists—and particularly by Shatby—in the protection of the spirit, of religion, honor and fortune, and so forth. Al-Haddad goes beyond the traditional concept of total intentions to a more profound one where "justice" becomes a goal in itself—complete, essential, and basic, encompassing partial details and segments, including belief and morals. Thus:

We will have to consider the big and clear difference between
what Islam brought and what it came from, which is its
"essence" and meaning. Islam would thus remain eternal just
as would the idea of belief based on *tawhid* or unity and the
nobility of manners and a sense of justice and equality
between people. Hence the difference between these
essential teachings and the transient conditions of humanity
and the state of mind deeply entrenched in the *jahiliyya*, in
the age of ignorance prior to Islam. Thus, if conditions are
not appropriate for the existence of certain rulings, they will
disappear with the disappearance of the former. If some of
these conditions cease to exist, this will not damage Islam as,
for instance, the whole question of slavery, concubines,
polygamy and many such conditions which cannot be
considered an indivisible part of Islam (12–13).

Seeking the "goal" by way of the incidental and changeable
is the guarantor to presenting a legitimate reading of
religious texts, an objective reading in the sense of a relative
historical reading. With changing conditions and
circumstances, we need to have re-reading based on
something immutable, which is the essential goal of the
Shari'a. It is in this sense that the questions posed by al-
Tahir al-Haddad acquire their legality as they are essential
questions to help uncover that which is constant within the
texts. We can pose the question in a more general way by
asking: Has Islam come for the sake of such and such? So we
can ask, for instance, has Islam come to condone the spirit of
criminality? Or has Islam come to exact punishment for
these people and for their actions? Is Islam a proponent of
equality based on what everyone in fact does or has Islam
come to relegate women in their femininity to an inferior
position vis-à-vis men and the rights given by their
masculinity? Has Islam come to sanction procreation so that
families and nations may grow or has Islam come to give a
free hand to men in matters of divorce, divorce that is subject
to whims? There is no doubt that the difference is clear in
the answers for those who have looked seriously into Islam.

And in that manner we can seek a pure Islam and distinguish that Islam from its surrounding conditions and protect ourselves from confusing issues.

It is obvious that these questions that seek to reach the "essence" of Islam do not only pertain to the texts that deal with women. They are relevant to all the rulings in the texts. On the other hand, these questions are conditioned by the nature of the social, political, and intellectual framework that delimits them. Thus these questions can change accordingly and we can ask new questions. This therefore means that the essence of Islam is not an immutable given but is one that is constantly subject to inference and to rediscovery in tandem with the growth and development of human consciousness. Thus we return to the basic root, the root of the unity of knowledge as it appears in the discourse of the Nahda that permits the mind constant free movement without limiting barriers isolating the constant from the changeable or the secular from the religious. If one must seek the "source," one can find it in the secular discourse of the Nahda that refers to the "social" which, in turn, refers to knowledge, not in a dialectical downward movement but rather in a true dialectical relationship.

This explains the divisions of al-Tahir al-Haddad's study into "*Shari'a*" and "Society." He began with a section on *Shari'a* in order to show that the rules of *Shari'a* found their roots in society. On the other hand, by beginning with *Shari'a*, he intends to pull the rug from under the feet of those who represent the opposing discourse, those who do not find within *Shari'a* anything other than its literal rulings and hence ask for its absolute and unconditional application. The fundamentalists render this the means of salvation and the only way to extricate themselves from the crisis. But in fact, through their discourse they participate in deepening the crisis by consolidating that condition through an erroneous reading of the texts:

For the bad luck of Muslims—and I do not say Islam—the majority of Islamic scholars and *fuqaha* have not observed Islam in its evolvement vis-à-vis women... What the scholars have done is open the way for shortcomings to grow more and more and, particularly in matter of rulings, the differences have been magnified in life. It is clearly shown here that the historical predisposition of Arabs and all Muslims where women are concerned has superseded what Islam meant for them by way of sympathy and appreciation. This is not the first time Muslim scholars, or scholars of Islam, have worked contrary to what Islam has meant them to do (109).

We therefore discover that the woman question and the religious texts that pertain to it became an incentive, among many other incentives, for the Nahda discourse to come closer to producing a scientific consciousness and understanding of religion and religious texts. The mistake of the scholars of Islam or the Muslim scholars from the point of view of this discourse emanates from their failure to understand this consciousness. Their mistake with reference to the particular judgments or rulings pertaining to women is not their only mistake. It is a mistake in one direction but it represents an example of a more general mistake, namely, isolating the religious from the secular (the basis of the religious is faith whereas the basis of the secular is the mind) while, at the same time, calling for political equality between them. The discrepancy reaches the point of contradiction in the political slogan Islam is Din wa Dawla, (literally, Islam is both religion and state) that is, a religion and government, attempts to make the state subservient to religion, that is, rendering it into a theocracy. A theocracy means dictatorship in its worst form; it is a dictatorship that postulates that he who dissents would be accused of apostasy and heresy and would have to submit to rules of *riddah* (apostasy) and so forth.

Within the discourse of the Nahda, the disparate becomes unified for the part has no value outside the system. Demeaning women is part of the larger picture of demeaning human beings. Human beings are only disdained in a society that is ruled by someone who claims metaphysical rights.

> If we denigrate women and do not care about the backward condition in which they find themselves, this becomes part of the denigration of all of us and signals our acceptance of the conditions of decadence and destitution in which we find ourselves. But, on the other hand, if we love and respect women and work toward allowing them to fulfill themselves this is a reflection of our love and respect for ourselves and an attempt at a more complete realization of our own selves (al-Haddad 5).

"It is not possible that women fall and men rise. This is a clear fact that our minds have so far not been able to grasp" (al-Haddad 189). This synopsis of the core of the Nahda discourse provides an image that grows and deepens as we follow it. It stands against discrimination on the basis of religion, ethnicity, or sect. Magnifying it even more, to resist the duality of the "self" and the "other," means resisting the contradiction in which we see Islam as the "self" and Europe the "other."

In the opposing sectarian discourse that carries the slogan of Islam, all the images are reversed. The "self" grows exponentially in a compensatory move to make up for defeat, backwardness, and deterioration, and identity is determined along the lines of religion. The "other" is persecuted and, at the same time, women are besieged within the *hijab* and so forth. If we have tried to explain the reason behind the growth of the sectarian discourse in the light of certain conditions, namely the change in the international climate and its effect on the continuing state of defeat since 1967, this explanation becomes *"tafsir"* (interpretation) and does not, under any circumstance, aim at becoming *"tabrir"* (present as proof). If the discourse of the Nahda has suffered and continue to suffer form the impact of all that, the solution for breaking away from its state of siege is not to offer capitulations of any sort but to attempt to accomplish more, by relying on the one hand on the essence of earlier historical accomplishments, on the other, on the accomplishments of the human mind in all fields of knowledge.

CHAPTER SEVEN

Nabawiyya Musa and al-Tahir al-Haddad in a Virtual Debate With Anwar al-Guindi

abawiyya Musa was one of the early pioneers of the emancipation of women, calling for women's education and rights in the workplace. She was born in 1886 and lived to enjoy the fruits of her tireless activism until 1951. She was always breaking new ground: the first young woman to obtain a high school degree known as the "baccalaureate," the first woman to be appointed to teach high school Arabic, the first woman principal of a school, and one of the very first women to adopt the issue of the education of women as her life long nationalist cause.

Her autobiography, *My Story by My Own Pen*, is a rare window into the life of a feminist whose life spanned three-quarters of a century, an era that proved pivotal to the emancipation of women not only in Egypt but in the Arab world at large. Nabawiyya was invited, in her capacity as principal and teacher of Arabic, to lecture in Arabic on diverse cultural topics at Cairo University (probably another first). She is often associated with that elite group of men and women who were instrumental in the success of the establishment of that university. (This was at the behest of Hoda Sha'arawi, a leading Egyptian feminist who instituted these lecture series as early as 1910, initially in French.) Other outstanding women, such as Malak Hifni Nassif, were invited to lecture about the history of women.

Nabawiyya Musa, then principal of a teacher's college, lectured in Arabic.

Although she was never an official member of any political party that advocated the adoption of western values (as many of the leading intelligentsia of the time were), she had strong connections to Hisb al Umma (Nationalist Party), and later Hisb al Ahrar al Dusturiyyin (Liberal Constitutionalists), which subsequently replaced it. Her memoirs, her editorials in her magazine *Al Fatah* (Young woman), and her 1923 landmark book *Al Mar'aa wa al 'Amal* (Woman and Labor) all upheld the goals of these political parties.

Woman and Labor, her best known work, calls for the participation of women in the work place as a prerequisite for her emancipation. She called for women to join the work force in every field. According to her, women should not be restricted to careers such as teaching or midwifery. With the 1919 Revolution, the issue of women's participation in the work force was brought to the fore. The idea became more amenable to the public, and Nabawiyya Musa found herself naturally advocating for women's complete integration in the public domain. In this seminal work she argued convincingly for women lawyers, doctors, writers, tailors, musicians, and, of course, teachers. Subsequently many women became well known journalists whose contributions were inspirational to the women's movement of the 1920s. The publishing of successful women's magazines gave women like Ceza Nabarawi, Hoda Sha'arawi, Labiba Hashem, Minerva Ebeid, May Ziadeh, Amina al-Said and others unique opportunities to voice their reformist agendas. Many of them did not limit themselves to feminist issues, but delved into larger social and political problems. Fatima al-Yusuf, better known as Rose Al Yusuf, founder of the highly influential weekly political magazine, laid the foundation for a liberal voice in the press.

If we look for a moment at some of the regressive stances of the late-20th century advocating the return of women to the home, her "natural" habitat, we can more clearly assess the invaluable contributions of reformists such as Nabawiyya Musa. Consider the writings of Anwar al-Guindi, author of several widely distributed booklets about the role of women in Islam. In a manifesto entitled "Muslim Women in the Face of Challenges" (Dar al 'Itissam, 1979) he states:

> All the statistics undertaken by the pertinent institutions show how women are inefficient, and that in general their labor does not contribute much to the nation. For women indeed have a specific nature, which perforce necessitates for them different areas and curricula from those of men to prepare them for their basic goal in life, which is greater than any other: namely motherhood and the family. Raising children and creating [an ideal home]... (74)

A comparison of the writings of al-Guindi with those of the reformist feminists (men and women) of the early part of the 20th century illustrates both the precariousness of the current situation and exactly how enlightened that unique group of women and men were.

The importance and danger of writers like al-Guindi is obvious; his work is widely distributed in cheap editions. That is why in recent years there has been a concerted effort from official institutions such as the General Egyptian Book Organization to reprint and sell the works of the pioneers of the Enlightenment (*al-tanwir*) at nominal prices in an effort to counter such retrograde but highly influential tracts.

✕⊷✕

Three areas that seem to have evoked much debate both at the start of the century and today can be categorized as follows: women and labor; women and the veil (hijab); and women and education. If for the sake of argument we establish a virtual conversation between representatives of the pioneering feminists of yesteryear and one of today's commentators, we can perhaps better assess the contributions of those early pioneers.

The work of al-Tahir al-Haddad, an equally important figure in the movement for the emancipation of women, has been largely understudied, certainly in the West. He is remarkable in his avant-garde stances. Born in Tunisia in 1899, he had a traditional educational background, studying at the Zeitouna Mosque and graduating in 1920. A poet of some stature, he became especially active in the labor movement and his country's resistance to the French occupier. He wrote two books, *Al 'Ummal al Tunisiuun* (The Tunisian Workers) and his seminal work, *Al Mar'aa fi al Shari'a wa al Mujtam'a* (Women in Shari'a Law and Society). This, his best known work, which was written almost 30 years after the landmark work of Qasim Amin (*Fi Tahrir al Mar'aa*, 1901), remains a relatively unexplored yet pivotal work in the corpus of reformist literature. Al-Haddad's discourse, which grounds the discussion within Sharia'a law is crucial in understanding today's different fundamentalist currents in a different light.

Both Nabawiyya and al-Haddad were faced with vicious resistance and paid a hefty price for their pioneering stances in the early decades of the 20th century. Nabawiyya, for instance, was fired from her job as principal in 1926. The British colonialists had prior to that evacuated her from Alexandria to Cairo in a special train claiming her a threat and danger to their colonial aspirations. She subsequently took some officials in the Ministry of Education to court and proved their collaboration with their British counterparts. She was relieved of her position definitively thus paying dearly for her progressive stances.[1]

As if he were engaged in a virtual dialogue with al-Guindi, writing in 1930 back to the future, Al-Haddad insists in his seminal work that women "should study mathematics, physics, so that her mind will become enlightened with logic." He further adds that this will help erase the superstitious and benighted beliefs that for instance claimed that

> rain poured forth from under a throne in heaven...and that thunder was a mute king, and that magic and magicians held all the answers. If women were to be educated they would also benefit their children in forming their future, the children who in turn will ultimately benefit their country (205).

Similarly, a decade earlier (and nearly a half century before al-Guindi's calls for women's return to incarceration) Nabawiyya Musa fearlessly wrote:

> It is not enough to encourage women to open windows to enjoy fresh air. She should learn useful information about physics and chemistry. Women should be instructed in the nature of air and its specificity, and its impact on the body...It is not enough to teach her to polish her utensils and avoid the rust in copper and brass, and to be made aware of the dangers of carbon dioxide emanating from gas lamps without teaching her the basic sciences. All the advice will have no effect unless we address her mind before her heart (80–81).

If these stances by Nabawiyya Musa and al-Haddad sound today rather straightforward, they are nevertheless light years ahead of al-Guindi's 1979 discourse.

Way ahead of her time, Musa was also aware of the dangers for women inherent in some occupations, such as the handicrafts:

> What benefits a young girl to embroider, which ultimately affects her health, and eye sight, and stunts her natural growth. The tiny stitches, her constant bending affects her posture and back... Concentrating on the minuscule stitches, different colors, in addition to the dust that she breathes in from the stretched out fabrics on the weaving machines, all greatly affect the lungs (80).

The recent protestors against globalization who cry out against multinationals who employ the nimble fingers of children in Asian and African countries to produce their Nikes and other sportswear have an earlier champion in Nabawiyya Musa; three-quarters of a century ago she called for a monitoring system to ensure the good health of workers.

Nabawiyya Musa's words should be heeded even more so in Arab countries, who continue to force women into areas of production that take a toll on their health. She clearly states her objections to the employment of women and girls in traditional embroidery and carpet weaving, "for this kills her potential and talents, and moreover teaches her laziness. The young woman limits her thoughts and vision in a small sphere that is no more than half a square meter"(87).

Al-Haddad again and again reiterates the necessity of educating half the nation, "for there will be no success for a nation who desires to progress when half its citizens remain ignorant, and the only way out is to educate women. The centrality and importance of that cannot be overstated when we establish curricula (23). He admonishes his conservative countrymen: "Woe to us... if we can only claim pride in beliefs and heritage that we falsely attribute to Islam"(218). It is as if he were responding to a future al-Guindi, who at the end of the 20th century did indeed demand that women be repatriated to the home on the premise that the teachings if Islam required it.

> It has been some time now that voices even in the West have been requiring women to return to the home. In fact it is women themselves who are asking for it, in spite of all the advances, and higher wages, and all such benefits. This is in response to an inner calling, and a sense of a loss of identity.

With a rare sense of humor, and bitter irony, Nabawiyya Musa seems to be responding not only to al-Guindi but to all those retrogrades the world over who demand that women retire to the safety of their homes. "We cannot guarantee that women will always have a male provider as some claim. For presumably the providers are her father, then her husband, and then her son." She then bitingly adds:

> Have we signed a pact with death, who will guarantee that he
> will not steal the spirit of a Muslim if his daughter marries...
> is fate a guarantor that a woman will not divorce, and become
> helpless, or that her husband will not die and leave her with
> babies who need a provider?

Her arguments and the tone of her responses reverberate
across the decades in response to all those who today in the
21st century frame their positions in misrepresentations of
religious dogma.

"Women are noble creatures who are made to reproduce
the species," she agrees; however she points out that every
animal species is "capable of the same, so what is the value of
this definition" (28).

It is as if she were anticipating al-Guindi, when he
reluctantly approves of women working only if they are in
absolute need of providing for themselves and their children,
and in that case her work should be only in specific areas.
Her position on this point is caustically formulated when she
reprimands her interlocutor Farid Effendi Wagdi, who at
the time bemoaned the poor "American women who worked
and toiled in factories facing the flames of foundries" and
said that he "wouldn't wish such a fate on his country-
women." In caustic response Nabawiyya Musa reminds him
of the "poor Egyptian woman who groans under her heavy
weight of fruits and vegetables she has to carry to the market
place," all while putting up with demeaning remarks, looks,
and unwanted advances from impertinent men.

Al-Haddad was particularly outspoken against the *hijab*.
The question of the veil has been a vexed one for over two
decades and has been singled out in the West as the symbol
of all the problems with Muslim societies. Although it is
actualy a much more nuanced question, which has been
amply debated by anthropologists, sociologists, and
historians, it is interesting to note the discourse of the veil in
the early twentieth century. Al-Haddad unequivocally

rejected the notion of *hijab*: "In its present form it is nothing less than an incentive to seduction" (187). He situates the imposition of the *hijab* as a lack of trust in women: "It is indeed reprehensible on our part to intimate to women that we do not trust them, and that we accuse them when we impose material hindrances upon them (182).

Nabawiyya was also critical of the *hijab*, although she may have had some equivocal positions:

This artificial fashion, which stands for dissembling and cheating rather than following religious teachings, or modesty. Consider the peasant woman (*fellaha*) and her natural gait, is worthy of more respect rather than those who are covered beyond recognition (68).

She did however at a later stage admit that a form of the *hijab* was possibly protective of good morals and she recommended it. However, she hastened to emphasize the importance of teaching to women the "high arts so that she transcends the temptation of cheap artifice (make-up). Thus she will be protected from (lustful) looks by passers by, and will be modestly and respectfully attired" (20). Again her words seem to predict many of the arguments that women today who would not otherwise don the *hijab* put forth as a justification for choosing to wear it: they feel it protects them from unwanted advances in the work place.

Nabawiyya Musa and al-Tahir al-Haddad, speaking to us from the first part of the 20th century, articulate with great lucidity their enlightened positions on questions that occupied the general public of their time—and ours. They championed the rights of women to be educated, to work, and to be treated humanely in the workplace. Someone like Anwar al-Guindi, writing at the end of the same century, harkens back to a benighted view of Islam. And the discourses of these three intersect, as it were, in a virtual space that shows us the past is far from past.

CHAPTER EIGHT

Al-Sitt Hoda: A Comedy in Defense of Women

*T*he legendary poetic legacy of Ahmad Shawqi (1869–1932), Prince of Poets, in his native Egypt and throughout the Arab world, has tended to overshadow his equally brilliant contribution to Arab theater in general and to comedy in particular. Yet *Majnun Laila*, his poetic rendition of the time immemorial pre-Islamic folk epic of star-crossed lovers, and *Masr'a Cleopatra*, which immortalized yet another famous couple, Mark Anthony and Cleopatra, in their final moments, have primarily survived in popular culture through their musical interpretations, especially by such famous performers as Mohammad 'Abd al Wahab.

Scholarly investigation of his work has traditionally focused on his unparalleled mastery of poetic imagery, elegant use of metaphor, and revival and renewal of the classical poetic tradition. *Al-Sitt Hoda* is a relatively unknown play of his last years, a comedy that was posthumously produced, to highly acclaimed reviews at the time of its brief appearance on stage. Sixty years or so later, the National Theater of Egypt produced the play again (in 1997) to rave reviews.

Al-Sitt Hoda is without doubt an early 20th-century undeclared manifesto in defense of women's rights. In this very last play he wrote, Shawqi was clearly expressing a personal opinion on the topic of women's position in society and her rights. He reveals in this play a remarkable understanding of women's dilemma and is clearly sympathetic to her plight. Critics like Eric Bentley have warned us against the error of conceiving of thought and imagination as two separate elements of a work of art.

In *Al-Sitt Hoda*, Shawqi depicts a whole range of human absurdities and follies steeped in his unique poetic language. His heroine is a resident of Hayyal-Hanafi, in Cairo's popular quarter of Sayedda Zaynab, where Shawqi once lived. Through his motley crowd of characters we are introduced to the middle class mores of the time. Al-Sitt Hoda is a woman relentlessly sought after in marriage by a succession of suitors, primarily for her fortune, which is thirty *feddans* (acres) of land. In many ways al-Sitt Hoda is a familiar stereotype of the middle class woman, independently wealthy and often unhappily married, who uses her economic independence to assert herself.

Despite all the restrictions of class and gender, al-Sitt Hoda more or less succeeds in negotiating her fate to her own satisfaction. An orphan, and brotherless, with no male relative to protect her rights in an autocratic patriarchal society, she maneuvers quite successfully ten husbands, by foiling each of their designs on her fortune. She disinherits them one by one, to their utter dismay, and outlives a few as well. Childless, she bequeaths her jewelry to the women of Hayy al-Hanafi, in a clear statement of solidarity with her sisters in their struggle for emancipation and economic independence. Though al-Sitt Hoda is clearly bound by custom to a fate of spinsterhood or arranged failed marriages, she emerges as a strong and determined woman who manipulates her men rather than becoming their proverbial victim.

The rest of her fortune, the thirty feddans, she gives to charitable foundations (*waqf*), even while making sure that her funeral will reflect her status and circumstance. Wise and calculating, al-Sitt Hoda had arranged to stipulate in her will that her wishes be executed by the Pasha and validated by the religious authorities. When her unsuspecting last husband hears of her final arrangements, and how she had succeeded in distributing everything to the last cent, he faints, after incredulously declaring: "Hoda showed me hell in her lifetime… Now may the Almighty roast her flesh in flames forever…"

The play ends with a choral refrain aimed at all the disillusioned husbands, and a few creditors who came to claim what they had coveted for so long: They are advised to "Go forth, eat and drink your claims…"

The comedy begins with al-Sitt Hoda, who narrates retrospectively her life up to that moment, focusing on her past marriages. The plot is revealed in the form of a dialogue between al-Sitt Hoda and one of her neighbors, Zaynab, who reports to her the gossip about her many liaisons:

> Much is being said about me. They seem to have no business but my marriages and divorces. They say I have married nine and that I have buried all my companions… I am no Angel of death. Besides it is with my own fortune, and not theirs that I married. These are my thirty *feddans* that have attracted the men, and also helped bury them. Legion are my lovers, and many are my suitors. Had it not been for my fortune, they would not have come knocking at my door and kneeled at my feet…"

In these succinct lines, Shawqi's al-Sitt Hoda succeeds in encapsulating the whole gist of the play. She not only sees through the motives of her suitors, but also unwittingly exposes her own foibles, her own vanity. The success of this social comedy lies primarily in the fact that it does not seek to moralize. It makes no pretense of realism in the development of either plot or characters. In fact it poses no serious thesis. The play aims at entertainment, by gently satirizing the foibles of its characters. It however strives to correct, through ridicule, the greed of the fortune-seeking husbands. The verses of Shawqi in the process appeal to our wit, humor, and intelligence. The laughter becomes enlightening entertainment.

"At a comedy," writes Plato, "the soul experiences a mixed feeling of pleasure and pain." Aristotle states tjat "we are aroused by perceiving the limitations of others." Thus comedy is more elusive than tragedy. For comedy is especially limited by time and place in its appeal. Yet it is impressive how Shawqi manages to make us share in the laughter at the follies and shortcomings of all the characters, including our protagonist, even today. In fact, al-Sitt Hoda is a modern woman (who seems to be from Venus) in search of seemingly unattainable happiness. She poignantly analyzes her inner self, while at the same time she is painfully aware of the seemingly unbridgeable gap between her and the nature and motives of men (who seem to be from Mars).

Her first husband, Mustapha "tall as a palm tree and black bearded" was her only love, because he did not seek her fortune. He died too soon, and she mourned him all her life. She tells us she was twenty when she married him and will henceforth remain twenty thereafter. She mourned him and did not think of re-marrying before five years had elapsed.

The coterie of her subsequent husbands covered a whole gamut of stereotypes be it in their looks, professions, vices, and flaws. So there was the lecherous town mayor (*ummdda*), the learned religious shaykh, the unemployed lawyer, the handsome army officer, and the well-known journalist, among others. They all had one thing in common: they were fortune hunters, who invariably failed the test. Those parasitic husbands just wanted to acquire her wealth. When the jobless lawyer asks al-Sitt Hoda to sell her land to support his faltering career, and pay for his drinking habits she cries out in dismay:

> Were it not for my acres and their yielding crops none of you would have knocked at my door. It is because of them that I married, and with their yield of cotton I wrapped in burial sheets my suitors and husbands...

At this point she is so disappointed and dismayed that she calls on her women friends and neighbors to join her in chasing away the culprit Armed with brooms and kitchen utensils until the ingrate is banished forever. When enraged he cries out that he "had never married her for her beauty or youth, and certainly not for the sake of her black eyes, but simply for her money." The wronged al-Sitt Hoda, because of her social standing, had retained in her marriage contract (al'issma) the right to divorce, a custom and right only the privileged few women enjoyed (see Chapter 3)—and she uses it, interestingly, on the lawyer. Shawqi seems here to remind all women of their unclaimed rights, which at the time were the prerogative of the upper classes only.

From this point on, al-Sitt Hoda assumes progressively fuller responsibility and control over her possessions, until the final act when she disinherits all but her worthy women friends. Her message to women of all generations is loud and clear. She seems to tell them to move out of their protected environment and seek wholeness as individuals. She also admits that marriage is possibly just a legalization of the deepest human instincts, and that whenever conjugal bliss (such as her brief encounter with Mustapha) harmonizes, it can create the best basis for happiness. Although on the surface Shawqi seems to crystallize a 19th-century ethos, his rendition of al-Sitt Hoda is remarkably contemporary. He was clearly influenced by the emancipation movement spearheaded by Qasim Amin, and thus engaging in the debate between the arch-conservatives and the enlightened intelligentsia. Shawqi judiciously couched his caustic remarks in the comic genre, giving us the laughter that bridges the two sides, and resonates still.

CHAPTER 9

Modern-Day Shahrazads

rom Masu'di to Ibn al-Nadim and from Tawfiq al-Hakim to Idwar al-Kharrat, Arab writers throughout the ages have tried to emulate, incorporate, and appropriate the most elusive masterpiece of Arabic literature, *Alf Layla wa layla* (The 1,001 Nights) into their own writings. They have delighted in a world in which magic is woven into the fiber of everyday life. But it is Shahrazad as archetype that seems to have held sway over the centuries, continuing to this day to excite the imagination and energize prose and poetry. This study will attempt to investigate how writers such as al-Hakim and al-Kharrat have experimented with new modes of writing, while incorporating that eternal myth of Shahrazad in fascinating new ways. Reference will be made to the works of two British writers, E.M. Forster and Lawrence Durrell, whose perceptions in the city of Alexandria foreshadowed the quests of al-Kharrat as a modern-day Shahrayar in the same city that for him becomes an evanescent Shahrazad. Alexandria (or ultimately Shahrazad) civilizes and mesmerizes the tellers of the tale, the multiple Shahrayars.

George Lecomte, in his preface to *Shahrazad dans le théâtre arabe*, wrote of her:

> La cime brillante vers laquelle se tendent et s'épuisent les ambitions de l'homme l'oasis qui excite sa soif, sans jamais l'apaiser, le point inexorable où se rencontre tragiquement fidèles l'un à l'autre son aide espérance et sa désillusion.[1]

It is precisely this essence of Shahrazad that entices contemporary writers, be they Arab or European.

Alexandria, the Mediterranean jewel, like Shahrazad is an intriguing, exotic Cosmopolis, a cauldron of emotions. E.M. Forster's groundbreaking work *Alexandria: A History and a Guide* is more of an historical docudrama than a factual chronicle of a city. Indeed the metaphoric levels to which he rises when describing his beloved Alexandria metamorphoses her into the torrid cauldron of cults of which Durrell writes. "This capital of memory" is persistently "princess and whore," forever elusive like the many Shahrazads of the *Nights*.

Like the many faces of Eve, of Shahrazad:

> She would never change so long as the races continue to seethe here like must in a vat; so long as the streets and squares still hushed and spouted with the fermentation of these diverse passions and spites, rages and sudden calms. A fecund desert of human loves littered with the whitening bones of its exiles (*Clea* 55).

I would contend that the odysseys of these modern-day Shahrayars and their struggles to come to terms with their identities are vivid chronicles that have been forged from the Shahrazad archetype and rejuvenate that myth in exciting and more complex ways.

Early in the 20th century, Tawfiq al-Hakim unequivocally compared Shahrazad to a locale—in his case, Montmartre—and the artist with his eternal quest to Shahrayar. This time, we have a Shahrayar who seeks, as it were, appeasement for his burning desire for knowledge, and a place that helps transform him from uncouthness to refinement, from brutal force to reflection and feelings.

Is not that precisely what Shahrazad in *Alf Layla wa Layla* succeeds in achieving? Having perfected her narrative techniques, the storyteller not only saves herself, but presumably all her sisters as well—and perhaps Shahrayar as well. In his study, *Les Mille et une Nuits ou la Parole Prisonnière*, Jamal Eddine Bencheikh points to the now accepted notion that Shahrazad's true function is what he called aptly "*gardienne du lieu*," or the custodian of the place, or space. In confronting death she stands guard to the cause by showing the basic humanity of women and men in the face of passion. She thus "humanizes" Shahrayar. This *gardienne du lieu* becomes through her infinite variety both the inspiration and the *lieu* itself. The writer/author/storyteller at times takes on the role of Shahrayar as avid listener of the *lieu*, or the city, and he undergoes a radical change as the mythical prototype.

Modern and contemporary literature, be it Arabic or European, is not intent on mirroring history as much as manipulating it. Elizabeth Langland, in her work, *Society in the Novel* notes: "As soon as novelists select, arrange, and organize the disparate elements of culture, the arrangement takes on meaning or value" (5). When al-Hakim or al-Kharrat choose to scrutinize their societies as well as their inner selves through a repertoire of cultural symbols, or through the archetypes of Shahrazad and Shahrayar, they do so in entirely different modes. With the autonomy of art, al-Hakim presents the royal couple in his play *Shahrazad* at a critical moment in their lives. He introduces Qamar the Vizir and the black slave who serve as counterparts. Here Shahrayar in his quest for "Truth" persistently asks Shahrazad to "unveil" and "reveal" her true self. His unrequited curiosity forces him to roam the face of the earth. He returns still not satisfied, yet mindless of his consort's infidelity. On the other hand, his vizir Qamar commits suicide because of his passionate love of Shahrazad. Shahrayar is immersed in his philosophical probings, while Shahrazad condemns him a final time.

This play first appeared in 1934, and al-Hakim intentionally refused to commit himself to a single interpretation. At first, he intentionally invited different, and even contradictory, interpretations.

He finally succumbed to pressure and in 1941 in a work entitled, "Le Pouvoir des Ténèbres" (The Power of Darkness), declared that Shahrazad in his play symbolized the "cycles of history, while the black slave, Qamar the vizir, and Shahrayar stood for the phases of the evolution of humanity: the darkness of ignorance, the attractions of intellectual speculation, the light of faith. (Qamar means moon.) These three characters gravitate around the Queen, the symbol of Nature. In the work mentioned earlier, al-Hakim compared Shahrazad to the locale of Montmartre while the artist was likened to Shahrayar who seeks to quench his thirst for art, knowledge, and the fulfillment of his desires. He undergoes the transformation, and in "Youmiyat N'aib fi al Aryaf" (Memoirs of a Country Prosecutor) becomes a sentiment and reflective being. Shahrazad is Montmartre, for al-Hakim, but she is also the eternal woman. She is Isis, Goddess of the Nile, who is believed to have declared, "I am all that has been, all that is, and all that shall be. No man has yet lifted my veil." Like Isis, Shahrazad has resuscitated her husband, as it were, from the death of brutality and ignorance of human nature. Like Isis, Shahrazad represents knowledge, science, and the mystery of creation.

Shahrayar, in the meantime, seeks to understand the secret of life. He seeks to go beyond appearances, as Lecomte said, "Une soif nouvelle devore son esprit."[2] Later in 1972, Lecomte denounces this propensity of Shahrayar to seek to master the universe, by showing that the man's anguish, alienation, and failures reveal the bankruptcy of his initial philosophy.

Many are the Arab writers who subsequently were inspired by the archetypal Shahrazad. Notable is of course, Taha Husayn, (Dreams of Shahrazad, 1943, a somewhat prophetic work about war and the advent of the atomic bomb). Other writers take on the persona of Shahrazad as a confidante. Zaki Tulaymat, Ahmad al-Alfi Attiyya give us humoristic tales, while Ahmad Bakathir and Aziz Abaza go from tales of exemplary conjugal bliss to poetic drama to one more time immortalize this archetype.

But it is Idwar al-Kharrat who gives us in his novels the most interesting, truly modern, version of both Shahrazad and Shahrayar. If we accept Georg Luckacs' definition, that the "novel tells of the adventure of interiority; the content of the novel is the story of the soul that goes to find itself, that seeks adventures in order to be proved and tested by them, and by proving itself, to find its own essence " (89), then al-Kharrat's *Turrabaha Za'ffaran* (City of Saffron) is indeed a classic novel. By drawing on the rich resources of the Arabic language and its literary conventions by astute implementation of intertextuality he creates a complex work of art.

Like E.M. Forster and Durrell before him, al-Kharrat rewrites his Alexandria as an overpowering, enigmatic Shahrazad. Here the city (Shahrazad) is to the observer as the tale is to the listener (or reader). The *Thousand and One Nights* themselves become the concept of storytelling itself. Al-Kharrat works within an all-encompassing Mediterranean tradition, embracing all cultures, religions, concepts. His is not a culture of exclusion, instead, like the *Nights* themselves, his world vibrates with the multiplicity of human experience. In short, he recreates the world of *Alf Layla* in a modern idiom. With great astuteness he weaves into his text past, present, and future worlds of enchantment and intrigue:

> In the elongated room, with the wooden boxed balcony, overlooking the terminal of horses and carriages, I lay on the Ottoman couch, next to my marble oblong table covered with newspapers, where I used to study... my feet slipped into the land of the *Thousand and One Nights*, and I entered it, and I have not left it to this day. I suddenly found myself in ancient times, and bygone days. I entered the palace of Shahrayar, King of Sassan, and his brother Shah Zaman

King of the Persians... and I witnessed his wife making love to his slave Mas'ud with her twenty girl slaves making love to twenty male slaves. Carnage and turmoil followed the kissing and lovemaking, and the princess Shahrazad descending from her Packard resplendent in its squarish shiny hood, right in front of the movie-house on Fouad Street, "The Mohammad Aly Cinema." The silk dress revealed beautiful dark thighs, which barely concealed their dark secret. The formidable genii frightened me as they emerged from their jars. I rode the iron horses on clouds and alighted on ebony and brass cities" (79).

In this breathless unreeling, we experience the layering of this multi-faceted text. The narrative techniques deployed by Kharrat in this text echo with the familiar ones of Shahrazad, and become the *raison d'être* of the work at hand.

Kharrat's converging of time and space is akin to what Mikhail Bakhtin, in his important *Dialogic Imagination*, termed "chronotope":

In the literary chronotope spatial and temporal indicators are fused into one carefully thought-out concrete whole. Time, as it were, thickens, takes on flesh, becomes artistically visible, likewise, space becomes charged and responsive to the movements of time, plot, and history" (84).

In the work of al-Kharrat, the confluence of the mythic and the real merge to give us untold insights into his search for the authentic self. Like Shahrazad, his city helps him discover, define, and delineate his identity. The philosophical implications that al-Hakim investigates in his Shahrazad, or the intricate narrative techniques employed by al-Kharrat, are truly what Gerald Graff, in *Literature Against Itself*, calls "The battlegrounds of the constructive and destructive urges within the limits of a culture" (8).

CHAPTER TEN

Ambiguity and Relevance in the Works of Khannatha Bannuna

A n in-depth study of the factors that delayed the emergence of the novel genre in the Maghreb, a region that can rightly boast of a rich and influential narrative tradition dating back to the 9th century, has yet to be made. Although the social, political, and economic upheavals that shook the Maghreb from the 19th century on were in many instances similar to those that shaped the literary renaissance of the Nahda period in the Mashriq, it seems that a temporal *décalage* had set in during which the burgeoning literary genres of the short story and the novel were overshadowed by poetry, the genre that has always enjoyed a preferential status in the Maghreb and Mashriq.

In an introduction to a series of essays on contemporary Algerian literature, *Dirasat fi al-Adab al-Jaza iri al-Hadith*, the critic and writer Abu al-Qasim Sa'd Allah underlines the great need for such a study and urges the Arab intellectual who seems to have inadvertently neglected the literary production of North Africa to remedy the situation. He tries to explain this silence:

> In spite of the efforts of the Algerians to break away from the blockade of foreign occupation, Arabic literature in Algeria took on special characteristics as a result of this isolation, and consequently modern literary genres such as the novel, the drama, and literary criticism have suffered (5).

This is undoubtedly true of all of North African literary genres, particularly those written in Arabic. Beginning in the second half of the 19th century, the West succeeded in politically and economically dominating Maghrébine life—without managing, however, to stamp out the Maghrébine cultural and intellectual legacy. In spite of sometimes insurmountable barriers set up by the occupier, the literary influences of the Mashriq infiltrated the Maghreb. Intellectual exchanges that created an essential continuity of thought and theme between the two halves of the Arab world increased ever since the mid-19th century. It was the traditionalist movement that held sway, with its adherance to the long-respected norms of Arabic poetry and its proponents in religious personalities such as Ahmad Katib al-Ghazzali and al-Mawlud Bin al-Mawhub, who at times seemed to insist on living in a past that refused to accept the imperatives of an imposing present.

After World War I, a so-called "Romantic" school took on a special vitality and gave a new identity to the writers of Arabic expression. The influence of the Mahjar school and the Apollo group reverberated in the writings of such pioneers as the great Tunisian poet Abu al-Qasim al-Shabbi, who set the example for other writers of North Africa such as Abd al-Karim al-Aqqun (28).

It is to realism, however, that Maghrébine writers turned with greater enthusiasm, because realism gave them unparalleled freedom to treat any aspect of their contemporary lives, however sordid it might seem. These realists felt that an objective, faithful reproduction of reality had to set aside the exaggerations and distortions of romanticism, which tended to view the world with the heart rather than the intellect. The Maghrébine authors writing in French between the two wars and after, such as Mohammad Dib, Driss Chraibi, Kateb Yacine, Assia Djebar, and Rachid Boudjedra, among other great writers, strove to depict the lives of the forgotten and the destitute. But above all they tried to capture the wrenching experience of the uprooted expatriate who was an alien in his own culture and who lived in a hostile environment. The search for the authentic self became the quest for these writers, the generation of 1952, as well as for those following them who began to write in their mother tongue and to lay bare perhaps even more poignantly their souls and sufferings.

The Moroccan woman writer Khannatha Bannuna appeared on the literary scene in the mid-1960s with several collections of short stories: *Li-Yasqut al-Samt* (Beirut, 1965); *al-Nar wa-al-Ikhtiyar* (Beirut, 1968); *al-Surah wa-al-Sawt* (Rabat, 1975); *al-Asifah* (Rabat, 1975); and more recently, a full-length novel, *al-Ghad wa-al-Ghadab* (Casablanca, 1981). Bannuna, a school principal, drew upon her experiences as a student at the university in many of these works. Although never explicitly autobiographical, her work echoes the questionings and rejections of her generation. Her first collections carry the seeds of the estrangement of individuals from their society and their bewilderment at the hypocrisy inherent in it. Her characters' lack of heroism is by itself a statement of her loss of faith in the society of the forefathers. Bannuna is a writer whose impulse is turned inwards rather than outwards. The reality she depicts is not observed and then recreated in a sociological manner, but rather is set as a mirror that reflects the drives, the flaws, and the deep anxieties of a society at large. Her men and women are constantly depicted as probing, meditative characters beset by doubts, guilt-ridden and insecure, and usually anti-heroes. These people seem helpless in arbitrating their destinies. They are men and women who grope for happiness but rarely achieve it, seeming to encapsulate the anguish and defeats of a whole generation of Moroccans in crisis.

To give expression to this world, Khannatha needed to create a new medium of the Arabic language to present systematically her philosophical and psychological probings. She is more interested in the Arab consciousness than in the material, external surroundings of Moroccan society, more preoccupied with what her characters *think* than with what they *do*. For this purpose she seems to have created an agonized prose, a new level of the language.

In an introduction to the collection *al-Nar wa-al-Ikhtiyar*, the late Allal al-Fasi, the well-known Moroccan littérateur, champions the cause of this "innovative young woman" and chides those who declare her stories "not short stories in the true sense of the word:"

> ... they may have a different understanding of the form of the novel or short story... or perhaps they thought it too much credit for a young Moroccan woman to write more forcefully than many who presume themselves writers of novels in our country.

Al-Fasi unhesitatingly places her contributions alongside those of Gide and Dostoevsky. "Her style is akin to serializing one's thoughts." Hence the difficulty in following and understanding her stories. "Her introductions (of sentences) lead to results, means to goals. The sum total is what constitutes the 'whole' story."

The Palestinian tragedy is at the center of Bannuna's writings, the pivot of all that shapes the content of the Arab ethos. In *al-Nar wa-ul-Ikhtiyar*, the Palestinian tragedy is the condition while the events which led to it are merely the symptoms of a deeper ailment. On the other hand, the "logic" of reality imposes the means of action. The consequences should be the inevitable one: *action* to erase these conditions and create a new society. The obvious limitations of such an approach, its ambiguity, and the dangers of emotional rhetoric are all consequences the author risks; yet she skillfully sidetracks these danger through a clarity of vision and unshakable determination and belief in the power of change. She seems to be most importantly preoccupied with the anatomy of the anguished psyche and the crises of the ethos of the Arab intellectual. Bannuna's use of metaphorical prose in consequently more like poetry or a prose steeped in metaphysical imagery.

Her writings reflect several interlocking themes. In the collection *al-Surah wa-al-Sawt*, the story "al-Waraq al-Muqawwa" (Reinforced paper, or cardboard) addresses both the conflicts and estrangements of her nameless hero and heroine as well as the menacing spiritual vacuum in which they lead their lives. "There is no true being—as long as you and I and the likes of us are removed from the true confrontation inside and outside" (11). So speaks her protagonist who is confronted by his interlocutor. He, in turn, responds by giving a consciously didactic sermon. "We have to be in the first ranks with personalities different from the ones pre-ordained for us... We have to be propelled forward with new selves totally divorced from the past, from all that preceded June..." (12). When she pursues her inquiry, "Do you want me to sever my relations with my family, my kin?" the response is unexpected, enigmatic: "Cardboard is one thing and your family is another. In essence they are like you; they have to own their things in total liberty" (10). The stories, indeed most of her narratives, reverberate with similar equivocations.

In a story of the same collection entitled "al-Layl wa-al-Nahar" (Night and day), a modern couple is lazily lounging by a swimming pool and nonchalantly tanning in the sun. Like Bannuna's typical heroes, they are drawn into a cycle of obsessive quests for rare and hitherto inexperienced sensations. They seem to attain this nirvana by immersing themselves in drugs and alcohol. They proceed to denude their inner conflicts and insecurities. These psychological probings seem to justify the lack of any plot in the traditional sense of the word, or even the need for any dramatic incidents to move the action forward. The apparent inertia symbolizes the state of stagnation that the protagonists are experiencing. Real form entails real experience and these people are precisely afraid of experience and action. The only logical way out of this emotional and existential impasse would be death or, ultimately, *action.*

Not surprisingly, Bannuna often engages in a sincere and impassioned diatribe against the immorality of inaction. She reverts to the glorification of a heroic past that could only be acceptable if informed by a fervent and sincere social and political realism. More often than not, such privileged comments seem to be supcrimposed on the narrative. Yet her astute and deft intermingling of the many levels manages to salvage the work quite effectively. "She had tried to move into his world in his circle of experience to discover those wonders, but death inhabited him" (16). Then without preamble she comments, "The Arab is still torn between his yesterday and his today." The women in the stories generally reflect much more forcefully the will and power to change. As the woman in this story says, "I had taken myself off the shelf where my special circumstances had forced me. I struggled so that I could through my sacrifices fulfill or even get to know what I was about to become." In the process, she notes that the man is not with her in this struggle: "He threatened me. I made it clear from the beginning that all that he offered me was essentially against me and all that I stood for."

Khannatha Bannuna here seems to subscribe to existentialist philosophy. Sartre, in the first issue of *Les Temps modernes* in 1945, wrote: "We are with those who want to change both man's social condition and the conception which he has of himself" (7–8). Sartre and the existentialist humanists' literary views were closely tied up with their belief in the social mission of the author. Arab writers since the 1940s by and large consider themselves *muntamun,* or *engagés,* and view literature and art as a viable means to lead society to reflect upon itself. In *Qu'est-ce que la literature?* Sartre further specifies: "Through literature the collectivity turns to reflection and mediation. It acquires an unhappy consciousness, an unstable image of itself which it forever seeks to modify and to improve" (136). Thus the preoccupation is centered on what man *is* and what he is choosing to make himself within the historical perspective. As Hazel Barnes put it in her *Literature of Possibility,* "Man cannot choose his age, but he must choose himself within it" (13).

Bannuna's orientation is the future—the specific future of her generation. She religiously believes that the writer must make a politically and socially conscious commitment, a commitment ultimately aiming at the liberation of both men and women. In a story entitled "Suqut al-Intizar" (The downfall of waiting), a woman lawyer who is absorbed in mundane, petty cases dreams of heroic feats: "I wish I could give of myself to every hungry and destitute human being, to every possible change" (al-Surah 89). Her sense of utter inability to bring about any change is a condition that constantly haunts her and underlines her sense of loneliness and alienation. This perhaps leads her to self delusion, to believing that she can serve humanity at large in small ways by tending to their problems and litigations. Yet she is never totally deluded. Her gnawing realization that she is ultimately helpless is further seen in her comments about her circle of friends, who have succeeded in dismissing the whole question of responsibility and *iltizam* (engagement) by convincing themselves that they are mere puppets, insignificant to history, enveloped in a cloud of numbness and lethargy.

Bannuna's characters, particularly the women, are constantly challenged to choose for themselves within the limitations of their circumstances. In some sense they are faced with the dilemma of opting for either total freedom— choosing one's actions and bestowing whatever value one chooses upon one thing rather than the other—or total responsibility. Her men and women are intellects who perceive separate, disjointed states, and more often than not are powerless to control their environment. The tension is caused by the intellectual desire to achieve liberty and to end the state of paralysis.

The characters in the stories are both spectators and actors. They watch themselves live self-consciously. The danger they run is the possible failure of their attempt to turn mind into action and intellect into passion. Bannuna's characters are eternally theorizing about their own lives. In her 1981 work, the novel *al-Ghad wa-al-Ghadab* (Anger and the future), she attempts to treat some of the criticisms that have been directed at her treatment of form and content. She quite successfully attempts to merge two narratives that intertwine in time and space, while she develops her characters within a more traditional linear evolvement of plot and action. As she herself says in a postscript to the work:

> I have (attempted) to fulfill the multiplicity of voices, diversity of backgrounds, angles of vision, that interlock and separate until they merge in unison when thought and action are merged in a dialectical relationship reflected in collective action that seeks change (266).

The basic narrative is a sort of *bildungsroman* that depicts the traumas of a young woman who comes to terms with her family and society and who refuses to accept the dictates of a society that tells her "be armed with beauty, knowledge is only second best (12). This avid adolescent is consequently "left in despair, loneliness, and the moaning of the sea, watching the vagrancies of the bathers, the pages of the unread books, and my father's principles" (13). Hoda, our young heroine, literally grows before our very eyes through her close relationship and correspondence with Salwa, her family and college friend. Salwa is perhaps an alter ego, or what Hoda could have become: "Let us attempt to live... living is the high price we have to pay... let go of your stubbornness and share life" (53). But Hoda categorically refuses to compromise: "I shall only be a true face, a face that lives its truth in clarity like a child" (57). In a classical vein she makes the father the butt of her anger and revolt. "He sought to hide from that world from behind heavy capes and worry beads and mute prayers and never declared himself to the world" 66). At college, in the engulfing metropolis, Hoda more acutely confronts parental hegemony and autocracy, now that it is administered from afar, and eventually breaks loose; but in the process she encounters facets of reality that shake her beliefs totally. When Hind, a member of her group of friends, casually gives herself to Muhsin, Hoda ruminates:

> This kind of negativeness filled me with deep sadness... it meant that any sharing is not eternal... I thought she had mastered her fate, that she was the sole possessor of her body... its only judge who lived her life in the open (67).

The constant speculations, parentheses, comments and the immediacy of another narrative, which simultaneously echoes the main themes of the basic story and looks into Hoda's future (as a college teacher engaged in shaping the minds of the younger generation) is a *tour de force* that gives more depth and dimension to this work. The mature Hoda has not abandoned her struggle to denounce hypocrisy wherever she finds it. "Teaching was the regurgitation of words and realities passed over by time; and the brokers, the highly paid bureaucrats who trafficked in their teaching positions" (86). She unequivocally states these rejections: "What do I have to do with a society that lives its lewdness and cries out for purity? Either it condemns itself or purifies itself" (91). Bannuna also uses the second narrative to comment on a subject dear to her and a theme that is reiterated in many of her short stories: the damaging effects on the Arab psyche and ethos of the failure to find a solution to the question of Palestine. "Palestine is not merely a national or historical cause; it is the uncovering and denuding of a state of total disintegration" (134). This lack of resolve is indicative, in Bannuna's opinion, of what ails Arab societies in general.

Al-Ghad wa-al-Ghadab is rich with ideas and themes that, in their diversity, succeed in producing a unified whole. It is clear and outspoken in its rejections, determined in its anguished search for the authentic self, and unhesitating about the need for action and change. The existentialist dilemma is fully lived. Hoda, after recovering from a hallucinatory fever, assesses her life:

> My room is of no consequence among other rooms; my name a plaque pinned on me against my will. What do I stand for? Madness that is rejected by those who are rational—or a rationality that is not comprehended by the insane (143).

Riding a train home to her little town for a family reunion, Hoda articulates her feminist positions, and the pain of her difference, most forcefully:

> My eyes rested on the woman sitting in front of me. In their book she is the one who has taken the right path, the triumphant one who has produced life. As for me, I gave my everything to nothingness. A stubborn refusal took hold of my whole being. I would never become a producing factory on the outside, while on the inside I am paralyzed and unable to come to terms with my mystery, unable to possess any clarity (151).

Hoda not only rejects parental insincerity, but also boldly questions religious authority that hides behind the symbols of religion and abuses its traditional power. She unabashedly engages an *imam* in debate and irreverently taunts him:

> I examined him. He had nothing, really, but his mustache that merited to be called imam... "What can you tell me about religions, about believing in the unknown, in an age of material challenges?" He turned pale (162).

In a perhaps imaginary dialogue she proceeds with her inquest and only hears him cursing her as an unbeliever. "No voice, no understanding, no nothing, no imam, no mind in my city... and I killed the dialogue that could have started between us" (165).

She comes home to a sick father and a mother who irrevocably belongs to a generation with which she cannot identify. "But my mother squandering time and effort before a mirror hoping to regain a face that she might have possessed, a face that had landed her my father" (171). Her mother insists that she attend the lavish wedding being prepared for her cousin, but Hoda insists on remaining behind to nurse her ailing father. Her father, on the other hand, struggles not to show his weakness and dependence. "A man of my father's generation cannot accept and admit defeat in front of a woman. Each pays the price, but where is the alternative" (181)? Hoda reflects on the human condition: "I want a world without prison cells. I want a drink of water after which I'll never be thirsty again. I need realities without contradictions" (198).

Her love for Muhsin provides Hoda with another opportunity to learn to understand herself and once more question her own motives. It is perhaps Sulayman, who finally opts for a secure position overseas, who can unemotionally understand Hoda and her dilemma. "A female from the third world, who has rejected her roots within the very confines of her city, yet stands immovable watching over the authentic pains of man" (207). When Muhsin, in dismay, tells her to give up the crusade she has taken upon herself and to accept to live like everyone else, Hoda somewhat desperately responds that "her existence is unconvincing," but "suicide is cowardice, sex a game, emotions a luxury" (245).

What then? Does Hoda (or Bannuna) leave us in utter despair and capitulation? Not so. In the folds of both narratives, especially the parallel one, the author's message is unequivocal. The hope lies with the younger generation of students whom she, as a teacher, is constantly challenging: "You are a future that refuses to become the future because you are besieged in a citadel of acquiescence in the past..." (240). It is with those young minds that migrate from the villages to the cities seeking knowledge at their universities that this dreamed of future can begin to take shape. While Bannuna's heroes and heroines are anguished in their quest, Hoda, at least, is dedicated to her struggle to make meaningful changes in the hearts and minds of her students. Bannuna's humanistic existentialism is truly a literature of possibility and of faith in the advent of better tomorrows for us all.

CHAPTER ELEVEN

Images of Women in North African Literature: Myth or Reality?

orth African literature of French expression has evolved a new sensibility different from what the generation of 1952, that of Dib, Mammeri, Chraibi, and Kateb Yacine, produced. That was a generation of revolt—revolt against colonization and all its consequences. Authors had written about the ever-widening chasm between classes, the abyss between generations, and, of course, about the total alienation of women in society.

Abdel Kabir Khatibi in his work on the Maghrébin novel, tells us that the dominant theme in the whole of North African literature—be it in Arabic or French, whatever the form or genre—is the search for an identity.[1] In this short study, I will attempt to assess the search for woman's identity as undertaken by two novelists through the study of two for their representative novels. *Les Alouettes Naïves*, by Assia Djebar, is an attempt to delineate woman as seen by woman, and *La Répudiation*, by Rachid Boudjedra, is another work in the long list of writings that depict the alienation of women in traditional Muslim societies.

The search for an identity is coupled by a search for new formulas to build the world of tomorrow, and it is the woman more than the man who incarnates the decisive changes taking place today. The sufferings and lacerations experienced in the process of transition to modernity are best represented by the many faces of Eve. Recent literature depicts woman as a repository of many contradictions—those who wish to limit her existence to the confines of motherhood and wifedom portray her as a wife, a sexual object, or a companion. Other writers, advocating the idea of her liberation, equate it to the inevitable emancipation of other oppressed segments of society—the miserable poor of this earth, the black person, and the exploited worker.

The new image is in many cases an ambivalent one. In the novel *Le Virage*, by the Tunisian writer Ahmad Fersi, Salwa, the heroine, is a bourgeois, beautiful blonde—the thinly disguised Westerner who "remains torn between her desire for real emancipation and the rigid dictates imposed by a merciless society."[2] The novel dramatizes the failure of Salwa and Adel to bring themselves to transgress the sacred values of an Arab-Muslim society. They remain prisoners of that society mainly through their own fault of placing high values on those antiquated norms and codes that govern their society even as posing as liberals and champions of emancipation.

The many-faceted women in these writings may appear at times as the aggressor as well as the victim. In a novella by Ezzeddine Maddani the heroine despises her tubercular, unambitious clerk-husband and bitterly regrets her missed chances of marrying power and money.

Boudjedra's *La Répudiation* is a hallucinatory attempt to recapture a childhood and adolescence rooted in an intensely erotic society dominated by women of all ages. The main thrust of the novel, however, is the oppressive, ever-haunting fact of the repudiation of the mother. Si Zoubir is the feared and much hated patriarch, the embodiment of the atrophied world of adults who lived by superstition, violence, and hypocritical Puritanism.

Through the deployment of a pattern of images and metaphors, the writer succeeds in forcibly denouncing a society anchored in myths and locked into a belief in purity and abstinence. The fate of "*ce lot de femmes sans hommes*," (women without men) victims condemned to live in limbo, fiercely guarded by the men of the tribe who alone are entitled to exercise their legal rights, is the subject of this novel. Boudjedra sets out to defend women at large to Céline, his French lover, and the patient silent listener of his narrative "Il fallait que je la défende, car elle était aussi une victime au même titre que les autres femmes du pays, dans lequel elle était venu vivre..."[3]

The writer is obsessively interested in recapturing time, and the terrible moment when his mother is faced with the irrevocable fact of her repudiation. His writing contains tremendous understanding and compassion for this inarticulate victim mingled with rage and shame at her submissiveness:

> *Ma mère est au courant...* (My mother shows no sign of revolt. She holds her peace... My father wouldn't tolerate any reaction. She knows... a speechless anguish (and) she longs to faint. She cannot comprehend her reality. Words remain numb.

This confrontation is immediately followed by one of the many animal-insect images that populate the pages of the novel, a device successfully used to illustrate the dilemma of the heroine. The mother stands watching flies hovering over the dish of the patriarch while he chews away unheedingly:

> *Je regarde l'une d'entre elles buter contre le suc épais qui se répand.* She watches a fly stubbornly agitating to extricate itself from the sticky dish. Mother takes pity over such vain agitation. The fly is about to die. Her heart is full of sudden terror in face of the ineluctable death of the fly.

So the mother remains alone facing the male's conspiracy, allied to the flies and to God. The atrocity and injustice of sealing away the life of a woman at age thirty—*"elle allait finir avec sa vie de femme"*—is again and again dramatized. Her catastrophe is shared by all other repudiated women, rejects of society who spend the rest of their lives going back and forth from the house of a capricious husband to the *dar* of a hostile father. They all knew what lay in store for them:

> *Elles rentrent dans leurs alcoves où on n'allait pas tarder à les assassiner à petits coups d'indifférence.* Their fate was to be ignored and killed by accumulated indifferences.

The mother was repudiated in favor of a beautiful fifteen-year-old nymph who, in the course of the story, engages in incestuous relations with the narrator's son. The rebellious son is irresistibly attracted to his stepmother, while being well aware of his own mother's anguish:

> My stepmother is very beautiful, but I spread the rumor that she is very ugly. This helps my mother go on living. Mother cannot read the correct time. Time does not exist for her, so how can she experience anguish if she has no notion of time?

The animal-insect imagery is intricately woven into fabric of the novel. Women are likened to locusts ravaging whitewashed walls—hesitant in their demeanor and constantly in search of their equilibrium. With this work, Boudjedra rebels against that society that sanctions the repudiation of women.

> To repudiate Mother, Si Zoubir based himself on his lawful rights and on his religion, while his wife relied on the abstraction of magical formulas; she was a child, and she could only dominate things through the intermediacy of another transcendence, the amulets.

A word should be said about the language of the novel. A staccato rhythm beats through the book, moves with abruptness and shock. A mixture of tenses creates a sense of immediacy and veracity. Startling affirmations inserted time and again act like a refrain to the whole work:

> My father has two legitimate wives and a number of mistresses.

> He wakes up at a four in the morning for the dawn prayer.

The hypocrisy of the father and society is manifold. He

imposes chores and punishments on his insubordinate sons. They in turn inflict suffering on insects and animals, completing, as it were, an eternal cycle. In an almost ritualistic fashion they exorcise their fears and hatreds, like the mother who also resorted to her versions of sorcery: "We didn't like to spill blood... the cavalry of the insects lasted a short time in comparison to what we had to go through in Si Zoubir's shop."

The reminiscences of a child and adolescent are steeped in the sacrificial blood of religious ritual. Hence the recurrent imagery of slaughterhouse, women likened to "lambs" led to the slaughter with blood permeating the whole atmosphere:

> The 'Aid represented the most terrifying of ordeals for they forced us to attend the ceremony during which many beasts were slaughtered to perpetuate the sacrifice of a prophet who was ready to kill his son to save his soul... we were hostile to all this, to emphasize even more our alienation... we were the disinherited...

Hence the parallelism between the archetypal father and Si Zoubir, with the sacrifice of the son and the rebellion against the tribe.

Boudjedra is as vehement in denouncing the symbols of new authority and the current attitudes of the new society toward women as he is in exposing ancestral inequities. In the course of the narrative the son is suspected by the members of the clan, who detain him and keep him isolated in a mental institution where he hallucinates his way through the story. Commenting about Leila's (his half-Jewish sister) attempt at suicide, he seizes the opportunity to lash out with caustic remarks:

> She knew I was aware of several of her attempts at suicide... this propensity toward liberty in a woman contained enough ammunition to ignite the belligerent revindications of all males, bent on punishing mercilessly all feminine attempts at emancipation, a concept that had become dead and the object of laughter. The whole country remained adamant, and no

one dared question this; women were to be parked, raised like silk-worms, then left to die in their white shrouds in which they swaddled them from the end of their childhood... (287).

Nevertheless, the story ends on a prophetic note with hope for some kind of reform. A strong rumor spreads that women were organizing in the underground, were planning a march, and had plans to oust the government and annihilate the supreme chief. It was believed they had contingency plans in case the spirit of the chief returned. They were determined to rid the region of his evil presence and influence.

Obviously, the political dimensions of this work are by no means secondary or marginal. But the interest here is in the writer's technique, which has produced a work possessing deep resonance and rich fabrics of meaning.

Assia Djebar's attempt at delineating women and their struggle to assert their personalities and individualities as human beings is echoed with varying degrees of intensity in her many novels. *La Soif, Les Impatients, Les Enfants du Nouveau Monde* are all manifestos for the emancipation and growth of women as individuals, as well as being great psychological masterpieces.

Les Alouettes Naïves is the story of a war—a struggle between nations and civilizations—but above all, a love story that reaches deep into the psyches of its heroines and heroes. For it is also the story of the struggle between the sexes, the long unresolved, often tenuous, relationship between men and women.

It is through Nfissa that we become acquainted with the workings of the mind of an emancipated young woman. Her myriad impressions are given through a stream of consciousness, steeped in a lyrical tone throughout the narrative. Flashbacks take us to the time when Nfissa was taking an active part in the war of liberation in the maquis. Among other significant scenes we see through her eyes the death of her loved one, a whole village being set on fire, and all the males being lined up for execution. We first meet Nfissa after she had lived through these traumatic experiences and has been successfully smuggled out of Algeria into Tunisia, where she resumes a more routine life. She joins the university and drifts into a circle of friends, a composite of a generation caught between two cultures, conflicting ideals, and a raging war. Omar, the intellectual, frets about his existence, its meaning and is never at peace with himself. Rachid, the indomitable rebel, is the one Nfissa falls in love with and subsequently marries. We also meet a series of women, Arab and French, with whom Nfissa interacts and whose lives seem to orbit in concentric circles around each other.

In this novel, Djebar traces the process of her heroine's growth. The phase related to the discovery of herself as a person, thirsting to assess the world around her, is dramatized in Nfissa's actions as well as in her thoughts: "Regarder les autres, et se sentir comme un regard qui dévore tout."[4]

Nfissa as an Arab is painfully aware of the plight of her sisters:

> All our women are afraid... this absence of the man on the outside they ignore. They who are so talkative never speak of the fact that they are afraid; they are busy having child after child to stifle their fear... but the fetus in their womb sucks at them from the very first months, entwines itself round them and they give birth to a humanity that is painfully diminished from the start.

Her perceptive insights are balanced by naïve, idealistic cries from the depths of her soul: "Why can we not in one leap cross the distance between liberty and suffocation?" (167).

Her bid is for an emancipation that is total and unadulterated, yet our heroine is by no means advocating a rabid feminism. When asked by Rachid, "es-tu une femme libre?" her answer is "Pas liberée du bonheur"—that is, she sees herself as one in search of a formula whereby, without divesting herself of her liberty, she might share a life of happiness with someone, on an equal footing. Her earlier answer does not spell self-annihilation in the loved one. Djebar tells us, "Nfissa, in the process of loving, didn't lose herself but rather awoke to herself, held herself high as a marble statue, but also a statue of clay that could be molded and take new forms."

It was this complex Nfissa who attracted Rachid, who himself was much sought after by Julie, the French wife of his friend Farid. All were members of the same group. Nfissa's intuitions and limpid character guide her through her stormy affair with Rachid, during which she matures and becomes a seasoned woman, without losing her basic simplicity. The novel is suggestively divided into three parts with the titles: "*Autrefois*" (The past), "*Au-Delà*" (The hereafter), and "*Aujourd'hui*" (Today). The action flows smoothly and the past and present are harmoniously merged, producing a coherent uninterrupted whole. The mastery of Assia Djebar as a storyteller is enhanced by her genius in analyzing her heroes.

Another important character in the novel is the girl Nessima: bourgeois, emancipated, beautiful, and perhaps, the counterpart of Nfissa. More than Nfissa she symbolizes the victimized woman. Like many of her prototypes, she is the victim of her education and society—factors which bifurcated her generation:

> *Dans notre éducation on a tout mélangé, la morale, l'Islam...*
> They have mixed and confused everything in our education—morality, Islam, political criteria, bourgeois norms. Facing all that, one has an immense urge to live, as if the many generations of asphyxiated women had bequeathed us with their lives to lead along with ours...

Nessima envies Nfissa's capacity for happiness in the face of devastating blows. She herself is desperately in love with

Omar, but cannot attain any semblance of happiness however hard she tries. Omar remains insensitive to her, another tragic figure who shuts himself off from "others," by channeling all his energies into intellectualizing life. Nfissa's pristine love for Rachid is not the uninterrupted hymn of love of a beautiful waif. She is aware of the discrepancies surrounding her—the war, the dangers her family is facing, and above all the moral sufferings of her Rachid. *"Etre heureux, de moi, n'est-ce pas un scandale?"*[5]

Omar finds himself in love with Nfissa and through his eyes we see yet another image of woman:

> Every woman has a moment when her whole being relaxes, when she becomes flexible matter and seemingly can be molded into anything, provided there is power, into a prostitute or into an angel—a wondrous and fascinating metamorphosis because of the simultaneity of the two poles... (328).

To Omar, Nfissa is more of a symbol—a "lighthouse"—who diffuses warmth and guidance and vibrates with vitality untarnished and solid as the earth. He joins Rachid at the front and together they discuss and assess their attitudes toward the war, life, and women. Omar is the more articulate:

> Must we resign ourselves to preserve the women mummified as they seem to have always wanted in our society? On the other hand, it is not the fact that they will learn how to wear elegant clothes, or walk as gracefully as the French, or head formal dinners and make small talk at receptions, Moorish baths, or women's celebrations that will change anything... (335).

Omar, more than Rachid, seems to formulate his ideas less subjectively, perhaps because he was not directly involved with either Nessima or Nfissa. However, it is Nfissa who embodies for him the ideal he spells out to a cynical Rachid. Rachid had left to join the fighters and left Nfissa behind, not knowing she was with child. She had not tried to tell him or

detain him, confident that he would return to her. Nfissa
sensed that Rachid was undergoing a phase of suffering and
doubt and was drifting in search of himself. When he met her
he had not hesitated to draw from her well and satiate his
spiritual aridity, while she instinctively gave to him without
realizing how badly in need of her he was. To discover this was
bound to cause her much suffering, yet her fate was to
encompass this ever-present dialectic of attempting to reach a
better understanding of herself and her companion.

The ideal woman Omar only dreams about might as well
be Nfissa, for it is her image that inspires him to tell Rachid,
while resting between skirmishes on the border,

> If one day you meet in your country a woman or a girl
> capable of being a woman, that is, I suppose making love in
> the light, and a little later discussing with you matters of
> agrarian reform, questions about your country, one who loves
> you and perhaps may be prone to not loving you anymore,
> one who may betray you, sighs upon awakening, salutes the
> dawn like our old women, using the same words... we
> demand that she comes from the same earth, from the same
> depth as you, and to stand against the same sky, towering... a
> faithful woman but not submissive, docile but not passive,
> honest and yet mysterious, and I suppose amoral, for morality
> is not for the true women spontaneous and at times silly, but
> intuitive, and with all this, for God's sake, not intellectual,
> especially not that kind of dryness (335–336).

Although these words seem to Rachid to be an outline of a
political program to be adopted by the revolutionaries, they
both realize how much the odds are stacked against reaching
such an ideal state of affairs. For it is they themselves, the
men, who will have to change as well. If women so far had no
existence of their own as people and were vacuums or a dead-
weights in the consciousness of men and of themselves, then
to change this, the men will have to re-educate themselves—
both their capacity for feelings and their sexuality. Then, the
women, too, will become capable of developing their potential
for spiritual growth and sexual maturity.

The anxieties and conflicts take on varying degrees of intensity. Rachid returns a torn bruised man, yet not without hope for finding compromises with life. Nfissa, who loses her child, matures in the process of rediscovering her new man. She will have to work on dissipating the opaqueness accumulated during his months of absence. For as Djebar puts it, *"Car je sais à l'avance que la guerre qui finit entre les nations renaît entre les couples."*[6] For Rachid, Nfissa was the *"alouette naïve,"* a term used by the foreign legionnaires to designate the prostitute-dancers, symbols of an outward downfall and an inner light, victims of social factors beyond their control, yet carriers of a torch of life and love. Thus he asks his Nfissa: *"Quelle sera ta danse qui te permettra de jouer et de vivre à la fois?"*[7] So their life will be the searching and, hopefully, the finding of new formulas by which to live under new conditions, in a new society. As a man and a woman, they will have to work it out, spell it out to each other, and fight for it together.

Our North African writers may be still grappling with their portrayals of women: are they still caught up in an image of woman that has been perpetrated throughout history form a male point-of-view? Assia Djebar brings her insight as a woman and draws on her resources and particular experiences. Boudjedra seems unable to transcend childhood traumas and is marred by traditional patriarchal despotism.[8] A truncated image of woman emerges, victimized by the misuse and misinterpretation of an eternal law. Nevertheless, in spite of the oppressive weight of religious sanction and social pressure, she is not without hope. The implication is clear that she has discovered her potential and is about to offer a rebuttal.

Literature creates the possibilities that may very well grow into actualities. Literature, we are told, is subversive because it probes the imagination and is not answerable to governments or societies. Societies have attempted to protect themselves at times by the suppression of works of art, literature, or any expression that presented a threat. Flaubert's *Madame Bovary* is a classic example. The law was not so much accusing him of sexual immorality but rather condemning his exact rendition of the "woman problem." Woman begins to be problematical to herself and others when her consciousness develops to a point where she sees herself as entitled to an individual life. Her fate balances today between these two poles—in fiction and in real life. Assia Djebar invests her with an independent consciousness and an individual life, while Boudjedra painfully records the prison society has made for her.

CHAPTER TWELVE

Masculine Ideology or Feminine Mystique: A Study of Writings on Arab Women

hile modern Arabic literature is beginning to find its legitimate place among world literatures, Arabic literature by women and about women has been relatively unexplored in the West. The last decade has witnessed a surge of interest in the role and status of women, representing a selection of views of both Middle Eastern as well as Western scholars, mostly social scientists. The main thrust of these writings was to show that Islam, contrary to general opinion, was instrumental in raising the status of women to one of equity with men in most matters, and that many of the institutions considered anathema in the West, such as female circumcision, are the products of extra- or pre-Islamic institutions and social forces. While it is an accepted fact that the rising status of women is one of the Arab society at large, not enough studies are exploring the impact of their literary contributions, nor the manner in which male authors have sought to explore, explain, and incorporate the image of women in their writings.

Male Arab authors in the majority, ever since the 19th century, have on the whole been emphatically for the enfranchisement of women. The man primarily responsible for this was al-alama (the Reformer) Rifa'a Rafi' al-Tahtawi, born in 1801 and credited for having championed the cause of the education of women. An Azharite student of theology and jurisprudence, he was recommended by his mentor, the great reformer Shaykh Hassan al-Attar, to accompany the first delegation of Egyptian scholars to France. Al-Tahtawi did not limit his activities to being the official Imam, but put to the best use his intellectual curiosity and alert mind to absorb knowledge of every kind. He read voraciously in the humanities, literature and sciences, and more importantly, he observed and recorded what he saw. His *Takhlis al-Ibriz illa Talkhis Baris* (Manners and Customs of Parisians) is a unique document in Arabic literature.

Unlike the Europeans, who were seeking new vistas and spaces, and consequently created the need for themes of escapism in the search for what Rabelais had earlier termed "*marchadises exotiques*," Tahtawi was more like an archaeologist on an excavation trail, intent on discovering the hidden alluring treasures of the West: its principles of revolutionary and liberal democracy, its humanism. A closer reading of this work reveals what Roland Barthes, in *The Semiotic Challenge*, so aptly classifies as "Not a structure, but a structuration, a text distinguished from the literary work, not a group of closed signs, endowed with a meaning to be rediscovered, but a volume of traces in displacement" (7). Al-Tahtawi was emerging from his "Oriental enclosure," and with him, ineluctably generations to come. His observations about Parisian women reveal an unprejudiced mind reading and recording the signs of modernity. Strolling through the streets of Paris he "read" gestures, behavior, and images. The first Arab to be truly an analyst of Western society, his mind seized upon, dissected, and reconstructed for posterity a whole system that was outside his own "*tonalité mentale*." Fascinated by the differences, he brought no value judgments:

> French women are magnificent in beauty, and they make gentle and amiable company. They always wear ornaments and mix with men in places of recreation. Sometimes they make the acquaintance of some men in such places, especially on Sunday, which is the holiday of the Christians and their day of rest, and on Monday night in bars and dancing places

which I shall describe later. This applies to both women of good family and to other kinds of women...

It would be wrong to think that the French, because they are not jealous about their women, are lacking in honor. It is ample proof of their sense of honor, more than anything else, that though they are devoid of jealousy, they react with destructive violence against their womenfolk, their lovers, and themselves in cases of infidelity. Their real mistake is simply that they let themselves be guided by women. However, no danger can possibly come to a chaste woman if left free...

In speaking of women's chastity, the causes of misbehavior have nothing to do with veiling and unveiling their faces, but lie in their good or bad upbringing, in instilling in them the virtue of giving their heart to no more than one man, and in harmony between husband and wife (quoted in Lewis Awad's *Literature of Ideas in Egypt* 42)

Nowhere do we detect condemnation or rejection, but rather an openness and perhaps even a tinge of envy. He accumulated and discharged facts in the positivistic mode of a 19th-century savant. Edward Lane, born the same year as Tahtawi and destined to become one of the greatest of Western Orientalists, is credited with having set in motion a movement of cultural interfacing between East and West, a medium used and abused by subsequent generations of Western writers. Laila Ahmad, in her study of his life and work, quotes his words as he set sail in 1825 on his passage to Egypt: As I approached the shore, I felt like an eastern bridegroom, about to lift the veil of his bride, and to see for the first time, the features which were to charm, or disappoint or disgust (1). Thus was the exotic romanticism that was to dominate both factual and fictional writings given wind. Lane's *Manners and Customs of Modern Egyptians*, a classic in its genre, has nevertheless, in its treatment of women, been very influential in maintaining to this day inflexible stereotypes in the psyche of the West. Islam, the myth of the harem, women, feature centrally in these works. Speaking from his vantage point of authority, few could venture to question their views. Perhaps "the women of the higher and middle classes feel themselves severely oppressed, and are much discontented with their state of seclusion to which they are subjected," speculated Lane in a chapter on domestic life (184).

Writers like Lane, Gide, and Durrell, among many others, orbited toward these gravitational fields of the East but mostly created worlds of their own, commingling fact and fiction. As Durrell says of his Alexandria, they conjured up, "A city half-imagined (yet wholly real) that begins and ends in us, roots lodged in our memory (*Balthazar* 13)." More often that not, European writings situated in the Arab East, particularly the strictly fictional works, feature murky passions and bizarre doings. Corresponding to the period of early colonialism, especially in North Africa, the "other" is romanticized to extreme degrees. Most often using the literary device of the journey, the landscape and the women (and their status), become focal themes. Be it Conrad or Gide, Durrell or Camus, these authors experiment with form to interpret the colonial experience.

x₋☙☙₋x

Generations of Arab writers in the decades that followed, equally enticed by the West, tended to exoticize or "Occidentalize" their experiences, somewhat in the manner of Western travelers in the East. Burton, Doughty, Lane, Gide, and Durrell and others created an "*Orient de fantasie*" to serve their own purposes. Taha Hussayn, Tawifq al-Hakim, Al-Tayib Salih, and Suhayil Idris, among many other Arab authors, poets, and belle lettristes, searched for an Occident which "promised infinite possibilities" and new freedoms, set on voyages seeking new "sexual spaces," sought a route of escape from the dictates of bourgeois morality of their own societies. In 1872 Tahtawi published a monograph entitled *Al-Dalili al-Amin lil Banat wa al-Banin* (Guide for the benefit of young men and women), in which he eloquently outlines his reformist opinions. He demands, for instance, equal opportunities for the education of women, which he assures his public, will result in the creation of a more stable and harmonious family unit. These were outright revolutionary political demands, and implicitly they constituted the first steps taken toward such a goal. In 1873, one year after the publication of his *Guide*, the first girls' school Al-Sioufiah was founded. Subsequent reformers such as Jamal al-Din al-Afghani, Qasim Amin, al-Tahir, and al-Haddad, among others, followed suit, reiterating the vital importance for the education of women.

The experience and example of Turkey and its movements of reform undeniably helped shape the women's movement in the whole region. Poets at the turn of the century vociferously called for the emancipation of women. It is to them we turn now to assess the impact of their message. Al-Zahawi in Iraq, as early as 1870, demanded that schools be opened for girls. In his collection "Women in the East" he denounces those who use religion to thwart such efforts: "They tore up precepts of all religions and served from them for themselves garbs of hypocrisy." In *Poetry and the Making of Modern Egypt*, Mounah Khoury quotes Ahmed Shawqi, that prince of poets, on his belief in the true teachings of the *Quran* concerning women:

> This is the Messenger of God who did not curtail the rights of women believers.
> Seeking knowledge was a law followed by his learned women...
> The name of Sukayna was everywhere...
> She related the Tradition and explained the eloquent verses of the Book...(127).

Hafiz Ibrahim cries out his disillusion and disappointment to the reactionary responses to Qasim

Amin's seminal work: "O Qasim the hearts of my people are dead...Even to this day the veil of their ignorance / has not been lifted" (Khoury 128).

Fahd al-Askar, a lone voice from Kuwait, denounces the custom of marrying of young girls to much older men:

> Alas they threw you in prison of archaic tradition...
> A cruel father and cunning mother
> Forced you to marry this despicable old man...
> How sad to see the flowers wither in spring.

Decades later, Arab poets continue to write on behalf of women, registering their ideologies and inciting their public to action. Hamid al-Iryani from Saudi Arabia published a poem in 1978, after which his newspaper was shut down for some time:

> Tear it
> This veil
> Discard it
> Tatter it
> And leave death's parade
> To join the wedding's procession
> And sing...
> Destroy
> Destroy fear with violence...
> Destroy silence and speak of hope
> Destroy the prison and the iron bars of injustice
> Scatter them...
> And ask
> Ask the holy sayings
> Who has decreed to draw night's curtains
> Over the face of the moon...
> Resist
> You are no flexible bow
> To be twisted at will.

Nizar Qabani, the well-known Syrian poet and diplomat who has perhaps more than any other contemporary poet become associated with changing attitudes toward women, has rightly been dubbed both her detractor and champion. He wrote poetry in the traditional vein, adulating her, even dehumanizing her, but at the same time he often transcended his propensity for traditional sexism and wrote memorable lines, which were often put to song, liberal concepts concerning male-female relations. Very often adopting the first person "I," he wrote of the urbanized Arab women, superficially Westernized, and her plight; he also pointed his finger in accusation at her vanity and superficiality:

You want
You want like all women
Solomon's treasures
Like all women
Pools of perfumes
Combs of ivory
A horde of slaves
You want a lord
Who will sing your glory like a parrot...
Who washes your feet in wine
O Shahrazad
Like all women
You want me to give you the stars from the heavens
Banquets of manna
Banquets of comforts
You want silks from Shanghai
Furs from Isphahan
I am no prophet who throws his rod...
And the sea breaks open
O Shahrazad
I am a mere worker from Damascus
I dip my loaf of bread in blood
My feelings are modest, my wages too
I believe in bread and prophets
And like others dream of love....

Many are his works that speak directly to the issues in the voice of a woman, focusing on man's hypocrisy and double standard. From *The Diary of a Carefree Woman*, he writes:

Forgive me sir
If I dared venture into the kingdom of men

Classical literature, of course, has always been men's domain
and love has always been men's prerogative
And sex always the opium sold to men
A myth in our land is women's freedom
For there is no freedom other than man's....

Nevertheless, as well-known critic Catherine Stimpson, in a study of feminist writings, judiciously warns us, "A male writer may speak of, for, to and from the feminine. He cannot speak except fictively of, for, to and from the female." Indeed, much of the writings about women, especially the poetry by men, were a search for an all-encompassing comforting vision of benign femininity. If we turn to writings by women, we note a constant effort to explore and challenge the harsh legacy of neglect and the difficult imperatives dictated by a rising feminism.

These writings reflect both newly gained freedoms and virulently persistent injustices. Arab women writers have raised high their voices demanding rectification of these unacceptable conditions. The Iraqi poet Nazik al-Malaika, succinctly and poignantly sums up the women's plight of benign neglect.

When she closed her eyes
No face faded, no lips quivered
Doors heard no retelling of her death
No curtain was lifted to air the room of grief
No eyes followed her coffin
To the end of the road
Only a memory of a lifeless form
Passing in some lane

But women are not solely preoccupied with their own dilemma; they, like their male counterparts, are committed to the prevalent causes and to finding means to end the agony of political strife within their societies. The Jordanian poet, Thorayya Malhas:

If I could reach the sky
I wonder if I

My hands will move the earth
But if I
If I could find a seed
A seed of peace
I wonder if I
My heart will weave
Garments of delight

Fadwa Tuqan, a noted Palestinian poet, focused her writings on the Arab–Israeli conflict and specifically the oppression of the Palestinians, after years of extensively publishing lyric love poetry:

In vain, there is no echo, no sound
Come back. Nothing is here but desolation
Silence and the shadows of death.[1]

And her celebrated "To Etan: An Israeli Child from the Kibbutz Ma'oz Hayim:"

He falls
Under the star that branches
A wild tree in his hands
A web woven with the threads of steel stretching walls of
Blood
Around the Dream
He is caught
Opening his eyes
"Etan," the child asks
"How long do we have to watch over this land?"

Ever since the turn of the 20th century Arab women writers were seriously engaged in making their voices heard. Quite understandably it was the women of the middle and upper classes who had had the good fortune of receiving at least a primary education, who were the ones who succeeded in finding publishers who would even consider printing their work. Although today the voice of Aisha al-Tarmouria or Malak Hifni Bassif or even Mayy Zaideh may sound a little *recherché* or stilted, we must realize that these "ladies of society" were bravely defying the prevalent norms, which dictated that well-bred women were "to be seen and not heard." Hence when someone like Nabawiyya Musa succeeded in publishing her pioneering *Al-Mar'ah wa al-Amal* (Women and Labor) and articulately took to task accepted norms concerning the incarceration of women, she was laying the foundation for the extraordinary changes that are taken for granted throughout the Arab world today concerning women's full participation in building their societies. She was also well informed about the universal history of women's plight:

> We should not feel embarrassed for our current state of ignorance and backwardness. But we should indeed feel great shame when women of other nations (today) work hard and we indulge in idleness, when they progress and we fall behind, and the chasm between us grows ever wider...There is hope for us, for we have also awakened from our long slumber and we are much better off than our mothers were, and there is great hope for us in the future.

Her outspokenness was certainly unique for women writing in the 1920s, although it was part of a general atmosphere of liberalism that characterized the political and social milieu she grew up in. After all, Qasim Amin's manifesto on the emancipation of women was in its second decade of print. The Tunisian writer Al-Tahir al-Haddad had also finished his classic *Al Mar'aa fi al Shari'a wa al Mujtam'a* (Women in Shar'ia Law and Society).

It is only in the 1950s that Arab women writers began to write enough fiction and poetry that, for the first time, it can be counted among lasting aesthetic contributions. The period between the 1950s and 1970s has been marked by a major intellectual current both rational liberal and socialist secular trend, which feverishly attempted to supplant centuries of stilted traditions. The Western model was to be both coveted and shunned (primarily because of the ills of colonialism). These contradictory impulses resulted in an internal conflict in the Arab ethos which, on the one hand, accelerated the loss of values and, on the other, failed to replace them with any viable ideologies. An almost schizophrenic condition prevailed and is often experienced in the inherent contradictions of societies striving to hold on to their traditions while at the same time yearning to partake in the spoils of the advances of that first world.

Afif Faraj, in his insightful *Al-Hurriyah fi Adab al-Mar'ah* (Freedom in Women's Writings), examines how the turmoil gripping the Middle Eastern societies in the last four decades is poignantly echoed in these writings (7). The Arab bourgeois class that emerged and thrived between and after the two World Wars had forever shaken the established feudal economic structures. Large numbers of women had moved into the labor force as well as into the classroom. Yet the built-in contradictions were magnified, for the cultural, spiritual, and scientific freedoms achieved by women were not matched by emotional freedoms. Arab women writers reflect on these matters more than anyone else. Because of their unique stance, their art provides a reliable barometer. For instance, Aida Idris in her story, "Waqi' al-Awham" (The reality of illusions), treats boldly these inherent contradictions. Her heroine heads a life of unfulfilled desires, falling in and out of love with totally insignificant men. Traditional sexual taboos are inferred through the use of fairy tale and legend. So the princess who permits someone other than her husband to kiss her is forever branded with an indelible tattoo that can only be erased by death (Faraj 8).

More than any other writer, Ghada al-Samaan emphasizes the dilemma of the Arab intellectual. Her heroes and heroines are split between thought and action, between reality and consciousness, between old values and new challenges in life. Heroines and heroes in the fiction of Arab women writers seem to be perpetually doomed to choose between an ancestral East largely steeped in superstitions and taboos, and an unsettling West that only offers the realms of existential angst (Faraj 8).

Like the pioneering generation of aristocratic ladies who took to writing and embracing liberal views, the majority of Arab women writers of the 1950s through 1970s belonged to an elite group of bourgeois middle-class intellectuals. It is only in the latter part of these decades that we read women writers who speak of the plight of destitute and economically deprived women, being themselves products of the same classes. Sociologists have analyzed why women suffer doubly as victims of agricultural, patriarchal societies. They have yet to explain the poignant crises of Arab women intellectuals who are forced to conform to totally unrealistic norms of obedience and chastity. Jurj Tarabishi, in *Women Against Her Sex: A Critique of of Nawal al-Saadawi*, reports al-Saadawi's eloquent formulation of this dilemma: "The main struggle revolves around unjust laws and social conditions that oppress women intellectually, ideologically, and sexually" (206).

Arab women writers are the ones who have forcefully drawn attention to these contradictions. Collete Khoury, for instance, in her novel *Ayaum Ma'hu* (Days Spent with Him), as well as the widely publicized Laila Baalbaki and her novels *Al-Aliha al-Moamsoukha* and *A Ship Tenderness to the Moon*, deal with these matters in what today would perhaps be considered quasi-adolescent rebellions. Outwardly, they deify the imposed taboos while inwardly they are torn, and hence attempts at self-realization fail. As Afif Faraj puts it: "In attempting to assert their freedom through an assertion of their sexuality, these heroines are in a sense returning to a traditional concept of harem psyche" (14). He points out that in these writings we either see reversals of traditional symbols—the kiss, usually a life-giving symbol used as an omen of death or separation—or again women are forced to recoil into their self-imposed cocoons unable to live their lives fully. He also draws attention to what he claims is a disturbing phenomenon about women writers of the 1950s and 1960s: that they could never seem to repeat their initial successes and bestsellers. Collette Khoury, Laila 'Usairan, and Laila Baalbaki come particularly to mind. Though many, too, are the male authors whose literary production comes to a sudden end.

North African women writers continue to write both in Arabic and French. Many have chosen to live in self-imposed exile, grappling with the well-known questions of alienation that their fellow male authors have had to face. For instance, Andree Chedid, an Egyptian of Lebanese extraction and the Algerian Assia Djebar, have carved lasting positions for themselves in French literature, as well as the overall patrimony of Arabic letters. Their worlds are beginning to gain attention in strictly Arab circles, and attempts now are being made to translate them into Arabic.

During the last two decades, especially after the setback year of 1967, Arab women writers have produced works that resonate with the aftereffects of the seismic social changes that have shaken their worlds. Be it Jalila Hafzia from Tunis, or Khannatha Bannuna from Morocco, whether writing in French (the former) or Arabic (the latter), they speak poignantly of their need to overcome the contradictions inherent in their positions as Middle Eastern women intellectuals. They are fully aware of the overall inherited conditions, which are placing their societies and world in such a disadvantaged position.

A new crop of women writers from the Gulf countries and Saudi Arabia are appearing on the literary scene and hold great promise for the future. Thabiyya Khamis from the Arab Emirates, Maha al-Fahd and Nura al-Falah from Kuwait write not only fiction, but also scholarly works challenging the status quo, analyzing the position of women in the Emirates and Kuwait. In her poem "The Ten Commandments," Thabiyya Khamis is openly critical of the conditions and hypocrisies in her country:

> Thou shalt not write the names in the sands of dust which
> crawling reptiles turn
> Into burning coals
> In the night thou shalt not depart a stranger like a traveling
> bat
> Thou shalt not lie, thou shalt not steal
> Thou shalt not tyrannize
> Thou shalt not commit adultery—
> No, thou shalt not and tenfold.

Both Thabiyya Khamis and Nura al-Falah were either briefly arrested or suspended from their official positions because their writings were construed as inflammatory or ideologically unacceptable.

Women writers and particularly poets have succeeded in producing memorable works of art in experiments with language, and indeed like the pioneer Nazik al-Malaika set forth new horizons for Arabic prose and poetry. Khalida Said, Sahir al-Kalamawi, Latifa al-Zayyat, Salma al-Jayyusi, among others, are highly respected literary critics even in the staunchest male circles.

Other writers are beginning to be known through the foreign translations of their works before actually being widely published in Arabic. Alifa Rifaat's collection of short stories, *A Distant View of the Minaret*, was published in English, but not Arabic. Coming from a deeply religious background, she was forced to publish her stories, which deal openly with sex, death, and the afterlife, under a pseudonym. Only beginning in 1972 did she actually use her real name.

In Egypt we find a new outspoken group of women writers who address their audiences through a multiplicity of conventions, forms, and genres, including the mass media: television, cinema, radio, and theater. The 1970s and 1980s have witnessed a surge in popular novels, women's magazines, and women's pages of newspapers, all of which provoked critical contempt and sometimes professional jealousy. Many of the authors have become household names and have created characters that will continue to haunt our screens. For instance, Sikina Fouad's *Laylat al-Qabd alla Fatima* (The night Fatima was arrested), which was made into a successful movie. Or the work of film director Atiyat al-Abnoudi, which explores the political involvement of women. A flurry of prison memoirs were produced: Nawal al-Saadawi, Farida al-Naqash, Amina Rashid, and Latifa al-Zayyat have all been in prison and have all written about that experience whether in memoir or fiction. Those works not only recorded the miscarriage of justice, in sometimes loosely organized narratives, but also explore an old theme: the bond of shared sadness and humiliation.

And women are more and more turning to the theater and proving themselves as forceful playwrights. Fawziyya al-Assal won great acclaim in *Bila 'Aqni'aa* (Without masks) and Nihad Gad (who recently died) wrote a most successful, prize-winning play, *Ala al-Rassof* (On the sidewalk). In it, she investigated the plight of a beleaguered society, personified by the heroine's poignant dilemma. Iqbal Barraka, Mona Ragab, Aisha Abu al-Nour, Lucy Yacoub, and Eveline Riad all make a living from their pens—one many say they have feminized the avant-garde. Radwa Ashour (in Arabic) and Ahdaf Soueif (in English) have written powerful memoirs and short stories exploring yet another aspect of the modern Westernized Middle Eastern women. They are more openly daring in their treatment of the taboo subjects of sex and homosexuality. The collection of stories *Aisha* by Ahdaf Soueif was hailed by critics in the West as a fascinating debut by a writer of tremendous talent; her most recent novel, *The Map of Love*, was short-listed for the Booker Prize.

For the most part, Arab male writers have treated women as symbolic of their link with the past, the custodian of tradition, particularly in the works of the Maghrebine writers Mouloud Feroun, Muhammad Dib, Rashid Boujedra, Muhammada Shukri, and Muhammad Barrada. For them she is primarily mother and wife, symbol of the fecundity of the earth. Yet they have ventured to investigate a more subtle analogy when they equate their traditional oppression to their political realities. Dib asserts: "A man who oppresses a woman is no freer than a country that tyrannizes another country." But it is the women writers of the Maghreb who more courageously tackle the dualities in the lives of their protagonists. They, more than their male counterparts, succeed in giving us adult heroines grappling with their sexual realities coupled with their social and political ones.

Writers from the Mashriq, aside from creating traditional heroines victimized by social and historical realities such as the women in the works of Taha Hussayn, Mahfouz, and Yehia Haqqi, be it within larger frescoes (the celebrated Mahfouz trilogy) or shorter novellas, have been also experimenting with new modes borrowed from the realms of the fantastic in an attempt to understand and explain the world around them. Yusuf Isdris is credited with having been an early pioneer of subverting reality to reconstruct the elements of the familiar world. In his stories "Bayt min Lahm," "Al-Nadahha" and "Halaqat al-Nuhas al-Na'ima" he depicts women in daring new ways.

Filmmakers are coming out with powerful statements, too. Muhammad Khan from Egypt, a rising star in the film industry, has directed a substantial number of very successful feature films which speak of the plight of women and their oppression. His celebrated *Ahlam Hind wa Camelia* portrays the deep friendship of two working class women who are struggling to gain their economic independence. The men, be they brothers, uncles, husbands, or lovers, are shown as weak, exploitative, and unreliable, while the two women heroines are resourceful, generous, and honest. Interestingly, these films are great box office success; they reach millions of viewers throughout the Arab world.

From North Africa we also witness very powerful statements made through film. From Algiers, such films as *Zawja li Ibni* (A Wife for My Son) by Ali Ghalem (later made into a novel) talk about a newly married wife left to fend for herself with her in-laws when her husband returns to France in search for a better living, or *Urs Musa* (Wedding of Musa), the story of a shared love and rebellion, are forceful statements not only criticizing state bureaucracy and ideology, but questioning time-honored customs that are deeply ingrained in society.

Most of these writers, be they men or women, advocating ideologies or demystifying femininity, are justly celebrated not only because of their grateful use of prose and poetry, but mostly because their writings and their lives have touched an anguished generation. Rebels in their own way, Arab women writers continue to create memorable literature. They conjure and construct worlds of remarkable people, ultimately helping us understand them and ourselves, and something, too, about our collective fate.

CHAPTER THIRTEEN

Women, Love, and Sex in Idris's City

*Y*usuf Idris's story "Al-Naddaha" (The Siren), in his collection *Mushuq al-Hams* (Ground Whispers) is a study of the effects of the glamour of the big city on the future of a peasant couple when, irresistibly attracted by the possibilities of the huge, engulfing city, the peasant woman asserts her individuality. The story also offers innovations in technique and delineation of character. Along with Hamid, the husband of Fathiyya, we are frozen with shock and disbelief, standing on the threshold of his one-room apartment, watching his wife laying prostrate on the floor, her baby sprawled next to her, crying hysterically while a man makes love to her. Idris is effectively using shock, a cinematic device to create that initial effect. This *tableau vivant* is immersed in an unreal atmosphere where, for a moment, everything is enveloped in darkness, although it is the noon hour, and a stillness that seems to linger forever, only interrupted by the hushed incredulous gasp of Fathiyya.

While Hamid stands lifeless, watching, but not quite comprehending what is going on, the man half-dressed emerges from this scene and silently makes his exit. When Hamid feels life steadily flowing back to his senses, it is impossible to try to figure out who the *afandi* was, as he got lost in the hordes of other *afandis* on the street. [1] The process of regaining consciousness of the whole situation and resolving on a course of action is methodically traced in the mind of Hamid, the simple peasant who had brought over his wife Fathiyya to live with him. The thought of killing her

occurred to him from the instant he recovered form his initial
shock. Here Idris is not merely dealing with a common theme
in Arabic, or in fact in all literature, that of the cuckolded
husband's revenge over his culprit wife and lover, but he goes
beyond to analyze in compassionate detail the innermost
emotions and reactions of the beguiled husband.

> If he had killed her at this exact moment, he indeed would
> have done so, not so much because she had betrayed him, or
> in revenge for his lost honor… never… not driven by anger
> or madness or hate, but equally, or actually above all because
> of his terrific fear of her at that moment, for she had become
> in his eye a monster or a venomous snake, he had to kill
> before she killed him, to kill not in defense of honor, but
> rather in self-defense (7).

Thus it is the emotion of fear rather than mere revenge that
is the central moment of importance in the first part of the
story. From there Idris smoothly moves into Fathiyya's
consciousness, and thus we get a silent interplay of emotion
and drama, consecutive and simultaneous. For her that
moment was the one she had lived dreading and yet had also
nurtured in her innermost soul. She lay there silently
begging that he hurry with the end and save her from further
torture of thinking or reflecting upon what had just
happened. For him, killing her is a *fait accompli*, and it is only
a matter of choosing the time. This, however, strikes him as
being incongruous in view of the circumstances. To him it is
whether he should wait for a confession or proceed with the
execution, knowing full well that he may not be able to act
at all in the end. It is this awaited end that preoccupies
Fathiyya; she actually longs for it immediately so that she
may not think more about what had taken place. She wants,
above all, to avoid Hamid's look, so we get two conflicting
forces pulling at each other, each one desperately longing for
what the other desperately would like to have done, but each
afraid that the other may not seize the opportunity at the
right time and thus be open to other possibilities.

It had to be either immediate death, or a miracle that would obliterate literally all that had taken place, and then life could resume its former course. And so our writer delves into the psyche of this woman, analyzing her naïve, yet complex, mind.

Fathiyya is like thousands of other peasant girls who dream of marrying someone who will take them away from their native village into the exciting city. Unlike the other peasant girls, Fathiyya not only dreamed about the exciting prospects, but actually worked toward realizing them, for when two eligible young men from the village asked her hand in marriage, Fathiyya did not hesitate in choosing Hamid—the poorer of the two—who promised to take her with him to the big city. Thus we see how very early she had already made a choice, asserting a certain strength of character. What really drives her to that choice, however, is not so much her reasonableness as much of a certain sense of inexplicable doom. Fathiyya somehow "knew" that she was destined to live in Cairo, this huge, fascinating, luxurious place, "where callous dry skin disappears and is replaced by attractive smooth beauty."

Hence, led by this mysterious call from the unknown, Fathiyya rationalizes her life and the "meaning of every sign." She feels that she was destined for something better and higher than being stuck in mud from sunrise to sunset. Her beautiful white skin was made to flourish in the city, for she was as white as one of the rich, beautiful girls from Cairo: tall and slender and bound to eventually gain good weight if she ate enough bread and butter. This inner voice kept her going, goading her, as it were, toward her doom. So she marries Hamid, and although he is only a modest janitor of a house, she is proud of the fact that it is a ten-story building. Her one-room apartment under the stairway in the basement of that house—although not one of the beautiful apartments she had dreamed about—was more than she ever had, with a bed and a chest of drawers and, above all, electricity.

Fathiyya mused all the time, measuring herself to her surroundings. It is true that her beauty was somewhat different. She was like a sugar doll one buys at Saints' feasts, and her features were certainly very attractive, and her nose could not possibly be mistaken for that of a *fallah* (peasant girl), and as for her mouth, it was as dainty as Solomon's ring.[2] The strange thing about her appearance was simply the fact that those fine minute features did not fit her fully developed, mature woman's body. She was happy to notice a change which had come over her Hamid, for he no longer was the surly, frowning, and shouting guardian, but had learned how to smile and even sometimes laugh. In spite of her fascination with the city, she could not quite explain how so much poverty could exist in the place of her dreams. This, however, did not dampen her spirits, and she was still completely taken by it, if fearful. This ambivalence is shown consistently in the story:

> And she, to a certain extent, and her husband Hamid, could not only resist giving in to the great motion of the city and have it treat them like the others...but this great fomenting motion could only frighten them, drive them to reclusion, or more specifically, drove her to seek seclusion (24).

She felt that the new surroundings to which she was confined, namely the room under the stairway, and from which she peeped onto the outside world, was her only protection from what she termed a "sea without a shore or fathomable bottom" (24), and she imagined herself walking on its edge; if her foot slipped but once she would be finished. It was a sea:

> ...which had a thousand hands stretching out, and with thousands of smiles like the smiles of sirens or deceptive mermaids inviting her, luring her into the waters. Yes they were all cunning hands and cunning smiles, even that tenant

eager with the money in his hands—and the grocer's store so close by—petrified her, froze her in her place while she would turn her head, trying to avoid the piercing looks, hoping for some kind of a miracle to save her from this situation (25).[3]

And so little by little Fathiyya becomes aware of that other version of life in a big city. She learns through her husband and through the underground happenings in their building as well as in the city at large. She becomes conscious that behind the beautiful facades, there is another Cairo full of scandals, shameful things and goings on, especially at night; she learns to differentiate between the "real sister" who only visits the "poor" brother left behind in Cairo when his family is enjoying a summer vacation, and the "real" one who visits the family regularly during the year.

In spite of these discrepancies and deceptions, Fathiyya's dream remains intact. Cairo remains the great coveted place, and as for evil, well, after all she thought it was to be found everywhere, for according to her "if evil, and slime and ugliness was in the bottom, safety lay in floating or swimming"(26).

And so she continues to "float," until she inevitably hits the iceberg. To the young tenant next door, an avowed Casanova, she seems at first as though she will be his easiest conquest. Actually she turns out to be quite a variation on his regular victims: he soon discovers that he is not dealing with a common case. Fathiyya does not succumb to his charms all that easily. He realizes that he will have to wait and plot cunningly. However things take an unexpected turn to the extent that he, who can get any woman he desires, becomes completely obsessed with Fathiyya, and the more she avoids his looks and the longer she remains confined to her room, the more he resorts to all kinds of machinations to get to see her. Fathiyya, for her part, becomes even more fearful, and her sense of doom becomes ever more haunting. After having adopted the colorful dresses of Cairenes, she reverts back to her long black *gallabiyya*, seeking refuge behind its respectful protective folds.

So our young bachelor tenant becomes more intrigued and more obsessed by this untouchable fruit, so much so that he resolves to either have her for himself or kill her and Hamid if either one opposes his decision. Meanwhile, Fahiyya feels confident in her newly self-imposed seclusion. She even thinks that she has triumphed over her sense of doom and that haunting vision of an *afandi* seducing her. But the inevitable happens; he intrudes into her cloister. Idris discusses those intensely lived moments with great perception. She stands there astounded, paralyzed as if struck by lightening. From being a sentient creature, she turns into one who has lost complete touch with life. In her state of shock she manages to keep her child from falling and seeks the bed's poster for support. Fathiyya writhes and wriggles, but only makes her aggressor even more determined and his grip more strong. She could have shouted for help, but this was her struggle, and having people around would only double her shame, for all was over now. What was destined had taken place; they would only become witnesses to her shame: that was the catastrophe. Idris proceeds to reconstitute the series of visual and tactile images that take the form of a process that contributes in the end to the finding of her new self.

Anger replaces fear as, for the first time, she looks her seducer in the face. She examines his "white smooth skin, those long, thick lashes hiding deep green eyes, those regular shining teeth and that mouth which any woman would have desired to kiss" (40). His smile is triumphant and inviting, a smile she has dreamed about for so long, a smile that invites her to sink to the bottom with the "slime and ugliness." Such are Fathiyya's thoughts lying helpless at his mercy. Yes, what she has feared her entire life has come true.

Idris succeeds in charging that one evanescent moment

with myriad impressions experienced in a stream of consciousness. Everything converges: her fears, her dreams, her determination to avoid the inevitable doom—all this is charged in that moment, crowded with thousands of vibrations and emotions. All she could do now was to beg him for mercy, to shed tears, to humiliate herself before him, but this does not last too long. Idris traces the change coming over her in an interesting correlation between the effects and impact of the city on her whole psyche. She begins experiencing strange things, as if the shimmering lights of the multicolored city blinded her. Beautiful shaven faces, expensive elegant clothes, numbing perfumes, wide open avenues, people gaily walking in and out of theaters, clean healthy children with their mothers, all this conglomeration of sights, sensations and emotions steal into her being while she attempts to resist—a resistance she soon had to abandon out of place, for what was unbelievable and incomprehensible was her realization that the horror is turning to pleasure. That which was impossible to believe, even while it was happening, had happened, and then Hamid opens the door and stands there, stricken. She lays there expecting, hoping that Hamid will kill her, and thus fulfill all her premonitions, yet she somehow knows that he will not put an end to her, that she is destined for yet another life. The author tells us how, like a wounded animal, Hamid spends the night in a vigil after having lost all the driving force behind his decision to kill her. Would he have done the same had he been still living in his little village? Has Cairo totally defeated him? Was he really shedding tears out of pity for her humiliation? With the first rays of dawn, the family stealthily gropes for its way through the darkness, a small caravan in flight making its exit from the indifferent, cruel sleeping city, which is seemingly innocent of what it had brought about. Hamid is seized by a wave of fury and wants "to smash those glittering facades of lit shop windows," "to

uproot its asphalt"—anything to lessen his pain (46). Hamid
buys tickets on the train heading back to their little village,
but he alone takes the ride back home, for Fathiyya
disappears in the hustle and bustle of the crowds flowing
into Cairo through its Grand Central Station. This time she
is returning to Cairo of her own accord, not in answer to a
mysterious call. Thus Fathiyya at the end of the story evolves
as a woman who has come full circle, who has stepped out
into the world, the real world, to assume the full
responsibility of her destiny.

Fathiyya is one of the most interesting delineations of
character Idris ever attempted. The naïve romantic peasant,
sustained by her dream, stubbornly remains true to the call
of authenticity within her. Undaunted by the wickedness
and treachery she discovers in the city of her dreams,
Fathiyya takes the great leap into the unknown by
abandoning husband and child in the search for her true self.
The development and radical change Fathiyya undergoes
takes place before our very eyes. Idris' skillful narrative
techniques make us partake in that change, however
extraordinary its consequences may seem. She is by no
means an aggressive or oppressive female, nor is she a
castrating figure as are some of the typical Hemingway
women. Even so, her husband is shattered by her actions.
Nevertheless he shows compassion and love in the end and
blames an external force—ironically, the same force that had
made him into a livelier, more sociable and energetic person.
That she leaves him is not so much because she still feared
he would kill her, as because she did not want to escape that
"voice" that had beckoned to that certitude deep inside of
her which she had in vain tried to quiet.

Idris's work is peopled with other unforgettable women.
The woman of the superb title story from the same
collection, "Mashuq al-Hams" (Ground whispers) is never
actually in the story, for she is imagined by the prisoner who

creates her, who gives her a body, a face, a name (Fardus, or Paradise). Yet she is the core of the whole story, the link to life, what sustains our man through his harrowing experience. The story he invents to justify her imagined presence in a maximum security section of the prison makes her into a strong women of the world—a participant in a man's world and on equal terms within it. She is supposedly serving a sentence for having peddled hard drugs. Aside from that shadiness of her public character, she is the center and life-sustaining force in the prisoner's life, even until the end when he doubts whether she was even actually there.

In "Bayt min Lahm" (House of flesh) a group of women, a mother and her daughters, are determined to fulfill their humanity at the extreme price of incest. The remarkable woman at the center of this story is the mother, who closes her eyes to what she surmises is happening in order not to deprive her "own flesh and blood" of the enjoyment of life. This is an extreme, unlikely situation to be sure, but Idris uses it to emphasize his point about the centrality of love and communication and its importance for the discover of the "other."

The middle-aged respectable widow of "Halaqat al-Nuhas al Na'ima" (Rings of smooth brass) realizes that she has to assert her existence, to communicate warmth and understanding, and receive it in return even from one much younger than herself. A "miracle" happens to her and she discovers, even if only for a brief moment, that she is part of a great, suffering humanity, and that perhaps she can do something to alleviate momentarily for herself and the "other" that misery.

Again in the story "Hadhihi al-Marra" (This time), the wife, although at times she may be the source of torment and anguish for the incarcerated husband, is his link with life. He lives from visit to visit, conjuring up her image in the minutest details when she is not physically present. This sampling of the women Idris gives us in this selection of short stories shows us a group of women fall squarely within the existentialist tradition. They stand for the search for the self, the seeking for authenticity, the will to action, revolt, the acceptance of the world and its anomalies, and, in the end, the very essence of life.

xᘒᘒx

Love and sex in general are low-keyed themes in the Egyptian short story. Aside from the *roman feuilleton*, daily or weekly serials in magazines or newspapers, or the very popular stories of Ihsan 'Abd al-Quddus, Yusuf al-Sibaci and other lesser writers, these two themes are discretely treated. One of the very interesting treatments of love and sex is Idris's long story "Halqat al-Nuhas al-Na'ima: Qissa fi Arva' Murabba' at (Rings of Smooth Brass: Story in Four Squares), mentioned above. The subtitle, "Story in Four Squares, " gives the form of the story. It is in fact divided into four parts, each carrying with the title "First Square," and so forth. The motif of the squares recurs in very intricate patterns within the theme, the texture, and form of the story.

The story itself is simple. A middle-aged woman who, having sacrificed her youth in the service of a much older husband and sons and daughters, now realizes that she is unwanted, unneeded by those same children to whom she had given so much. After their father died, she refused to remarry, and had thus buried her youth and chances for happiness. Her children now are all successful and themselves have created their own families, and thus they have little by little drifted away from her. Today they simply come to see her on holidays, and no matter how much affection and love they express, she feels marginal to their existence. It is this feeling that Idris studies and analyzes in great depth and with insightful perception.

Her dutiful children, now engrossed in their own lives, suggest that she visit the shrine of the venerated Sayyida Zaynab, as it becomes ladies of her age and standing. Sayyida Zaynab, also known as "Mother of the Old" and Umm Hashim, was sought by young and old for her miraculous intercessions and doings. One Friday she goes to the shrine, and there the miracle happens. By some extraordinary coincidence, from among the crowding hordes of people who try to come as close to the shrine and tomb as possible and hold on to the brass rings hanging from the sides of the tomb, a young man helps her, supports her from slipping to the ground. This initial contact triggers a chain of events that she will live to look upon as the most extraordinary of her life. There immediately grows between those two people, so different in backgrounds, age and status, a love relationship of a unique kind. It is here that the genius of Idris makes its mark. He analyzes and explains this love story within the limits of his four squares and the "Rings of Smooth Brass." He delves into deeper realms of archetypal nature. He touches upon the Oedipal complex and incorporates it into the framework of his story.

So this middle-aged, respectable grandmother finds herself deeply involved with a twenty-year-old motherless boy. The attraction is mutual, animal in its primitiveness, but also real and noble. Idris traces in an effective stream of consciousness the reaction of the woman to the initial encounter with the touch of the young man:

> By what force can she inform him of that feeling she can no longer fight, which made her forget everything but the fact that she had found him, and that at this specific moment he was dearer to her than the whole world (164).

This sudden, violent attraction of two people, who are both unloved, unwanted, and unneeded, is stronger than all the conceivable objections. She always reminds him, and herself, of the obvious fact that she is like his mother, and that he

should treat her as such. The young man, aware of the fact
but starving for affection, was ready for it from any source,
especially from a mother-image. This vital forced that draws
them together is shown by Idris as being a natural force that
she has disregarded for years:

> Since the call, a genii had awaken in her, capable of
> everything, alive, throbbing with life, a genii she had ignored
> and tried to kill, ignored by her children and all those around
> her, and by all the values and mores and advice that tried to
> strangle him, imprison him, until he died from neglect and
> want (174).

We thus see in action the tremendous change that this
restrained and conventional middle-aged woman undergoes.
She is fully aware and in control of her actions and feelings,
however strange they may be:

> Aware of it being a risk, she was confident that her judgment
> was right, confident that in the end she would give him the
> "mother" in her, were it only for a few hours, and take from
> him, maybe against his wish, the "son" were it only for a few
> minutes, and that she could never, never escape this fate (175).

So she accompanies him to his shack of a home and cleans
the abandoned place and cooks for him a hearty meal, and as
she would do it for her own child, bathes him.

> And what she had expected exactly happened, for the
> morning in her found the child in him, and the child in him
> brought back certain touches and features of her motherhood
> that had long withered and died, and she seemed to become
> a mother for the very first time (177).

Thus a complex relationship develops between those two
people hungering for affection and love. The mother/son
initial contact metamorphoses into a man/woman need, yet
it goes through a phase, as it were, of a rarifying medium of
deep love and emotion.

> And so, in spite of their close clasp, there started to grow and
> spread an emotional cloud that totally enveloped them, and

completely bound them, a cloud secreted by their bodies, to
excite all that is not possible for the body to excite. Could it
be love? (182)

So ends the first square in which the designs of this
extraordinary relationship have been drawn. The "Second
Square" is an elaboration of the motifs painted in the first
place. Here are presented the detailed analysis of this
attraction of opposites. Idris probes the depths of human
psyche and links this act to something primeval that reaches
far back in human consciousness. Their movements reflect
the primal desire of man to return to the womb and of
woman to absorb and contain.[4] Idris compares their
attraction to yet another immutable pattern, in terms of the
principles governing the solar system.

> Attraction generating attraction, this wide universe capable
> of suspending our planet, our sun and thousands of others in
> their frightening space with nothing but the attraction of
> gravity, and attraction of opposites, attraction of which no
> one knows the secret until now: that which attracts especially
> the woman to the man so as to use him as a means to
> reproduce a copy of her own making of that same man, to
> have a son, and how marvelous would it be if it came to be
> exactly like the father, and she would do anything for his
> love; and if it were permissible to choose that same son to
> produce for her, from her own self also another son: closer to
> what she wants and desires (185).

Idris further elaborates on this imagery when, in the Third
Square, he describes how this youth orbited around his star,
became part of her whole system, ineluctably moving in her
orbit. Yet Idris constantly reminds us of the reality of the
situation. He does not remain in these high spheres but
periodically brings the mother/son axis into play, for in spite
of her discovering how the female in her had suddenly
bloomed and flourished to extremes she never realized she
was capable of, and in spite of her giving of herself without
guilt or shame, even of the specter of her social being

believing the bliss she was experiencing. So the communion of these two beings takes place, transcending all possible obstacles, social, moral or religious.

> And between the two great poles a welding spark generated like a bolt, a thunderbolt that made the square tiles in the room tremble and the windows shake (192).

The fourth and last part of the story completes the symmetry of this mosaic-like design. Although a miracle had happened and her children marveled at her newly found vitality and her total devotion to Sayyida Zaynab, she knew that it would all come to an end. Eventually, the inevitable takes place: The young man loses interest in her and turns to a younger, prettier woman.

> She felt that she did not want to moan, and that she could put an end to her dizziness, for she was not sad nor reproachful, nor was she surprised or even bitter toward him about the girl. She realized through an indefinable feeling, without any begrudging, that she too had nothing to give or bestow, neither a surplus of motherhood nor an excess of affection: the green active volcano did not have one drop left in it (165).

With this sense of emptiness and void, she turns to Umm Hashim, Sayyida Zaynab, mother of the Old, for she realizes that from now on, she is doomed to a life of solitude and loneliness. She feels unwanted and unneeded and therefore clings with whatever energy she can summon to the rings around the marble tomb, rings that have themselves become worn out, eaten up by God knows how many thousands of people who, like her, in utter desperation had turned to the shrine of the holy woman, seeking comfort in their hour of trial and desolation:

> There she was like the precursor of winter, without noise she came... true loneliness without any kind of escape... a loneliness like a demarcation line between being a son and becoming a father. Her motherhood had been exhausted to the very last, or seemed to have been; her becoming once more

a child, a daughter to a mother that did not exist, maybe that is why she was named "Mother of the Old," for the man cannot survive as a human unless he be a father or a son. If his virility comes to an end, he resumes being a son. And if mother hood is no more, the woman becomes a daughter once more, a rule without exceptions… But now she is in a decisive moment of loneliness, loneliness like that of Sayyida Zaynab herself, with people crowding around her, holding onto the rings around her tomb, men and women, each and every one lonely like herself, all with one hope: to return to being sons and daughters to Mother of the Old. Lonely in her tomb in spite of the crowds around, each one trying to grasp one of those rings, insistent to the point of tears and moans, and succeeding for a brief moment in leaving his state of loneliness and touching his mother, mother of all, she may be, but in spite of everything, she is lonely (197).

What Idris was attempting in his portrayal of this woman was something beyond the sensuous or incestuously carnal. He was trying to objectify as forcefully as possible the intrinsic needs of human beings, needs that transcend all the norms of recognized behavior, propriety, and decorum. The need for compassion and love, pure and simple, is the main thrust of this piece of literature. Idris the artist catalyzes this through the medium of his art and vision. He immerses it in a media of local color but never drowns his characters. They retain a universal appeal because of the humanity that transpires in every word and action.

One of Idris' most startling and daring stories in the realm of sex, the title story of *Bayt min Lahm* (House of Flesh), is an extreme indictment of the same human needs shown by the characters in "The Rings of Smooth Brass." Here Idris uses great economy in transmitting the contents of the story. The motif of silence, which underlies the whole structure of the story, is thus integrated in the texture and form. The compactness and economy of the narrative also serves as an objective correlation to the paucity of feelings and the extreme emotional need of the characters at play.

A young and pretty woman in left burdened by three ugly girls of marriageable age after the death of her old, sickly husband. His disappearance not only causes them economic hardships, but most important of all, deprives them of contact with the male element, for at least when the father was alive his friends would come and go, sustaining their hope that maybe one day they would bring along some eligible young men. But now poor and unattractive, their chances are slim, and as the days go by their hopes dwindle and silence reigns over them.

The traditional silence that accompanies homes in mourning is interrupted weekly by the neighborhood shaykh who comes every Friday to chant verses from the *Quran* in memory of the dead.

> A silence broken only by the chanting voices... rising in a routine, with neither emotion nor seriousness. The chants were delivered by a Muqri,[5] and the Muqri was blind...and on the mat he would sit cross-legged, and when he was done he would grope for his sandals and bid those around good day, a greeting no one bothers to return, and leave. Out of habit he comes, out of habit he chants, out of habit he leaves, to the extent that no one paid anymore attention to him (6).

That life, enveloped in silence and despair, could have continued for those four women, captives of tradition, poverty, denied their natural rights and needs, if the shaykh had not suddenly stopped his weekly visit. Then they realized the extent of their loss. Not only was he the "only voice that broke that silence," but he was also "the only man who once a week knocked on their door." They also realized that although blind, he was young and carefully dressed and above all had a strong, beautiful ringing voice.

So they had to act quickly; they have to renew the weekly contract. It is then that they decide among themselves that they should not let him go. One of them should marry him:

> The girls suggest, and the mother looks at their faces to decide who shall be the one, but the faces are evasive, merely

156

suggestive, saying without words "Shall we break our fast with a blind one?" They still are dreaming of their grooms, and grooms are usually seeing ones. Poor creatures, they know not the world of men, impossible for them to understand that a man is not measured by his eyes (7–8).

In the hope of having a man live among them and therefore invite other male company to their home, they convince their young mother to marry the blind shaykh, who accepts willingly. For a while the silence seems to be gone forever. His strong beautiful voice reflects his newly found happiness, and the mother's newly found vitality reflects her new attitude toward life:

> The silence disappeared, as if never to return again: the bustle of life throbbed. The husband is her lawful man, according to the law of God and his prophet, so what is there to be ashamed of? All that she does is acceptable... even when night comes, and they are all together, and the souls; and bodies' reins are set free, even with the girls scattered across the room, understanding and comprehending, nailed in their places, imprisoning their movements and their coughs, while breaths and noises are hushed, and moans escape, only to be silenced by other moans (9).

Doubts assail the young blind man when one day his woman is fresh and bursting with youth and vitality and soft, and the next she is worn out, rough to the touch. But he too chooses silence, for he fears the inevitable.

> Maybe one word will escape and the whole edifice of silence will crumble, and woe to him if the wall of silence collapses, the different, strange silence that has taken hold of all, the voluntary silence this time, not caused by poverty of ugliness or patience or even despair. But it is the deepest kind of silence, for it is the silence agreed upon tacitly, the strongest, most binding of all agreements, that which is sealed without any agreement (13).

And he tries to make believe that his partner is always his wife, forever changing, versatile and unpredictable.

For this was the business of the seeing only, and their responsibility alone. They alone possess the grace of certitude, for they are capable of differentiating, and the most he can do is doubt, doubt that can only become certainty through sight, and as long as he is denied it, he will remain without certainty, for he is the blind man, and there is no embarrassment for a blind man. Or is there embarrassment for a blind man? (13).

On this doubtful note ends this intriguing story. This study of the different kinds of silence is also an innovative and daring questioning of accepted norms of social behavior. Not that Idris condones incestuous relationships; rather he forcefully condemns the human conditions that lead to such anomalies. The anonymity of the characters, although representative of a given segment of society, lends a universal dimension to the whole structure. The poetic use of "silence" as a recurring motif gives unity to this tightly knit story. The element of blindness, which plays such a crucial part in the story, serves as a counterpart to this motif and enhances it.

CHAPTER FOURTEEN

A Compromise on the Road to Happiness: Love in Naguib Mahfouz's Repetoire

aguib Mahfouz treats love very differently than
Idris. Mahouz seems to be much more
preoccupied with basic philosophical *données*.
Here it is evident that his own background and training in
philosophy dominates his vision. A long short story in the
collection entitled "Hikaya bila Bidaya wala Nihaya" (Story
Without Beginning or End) deals with a study of a
fundamental aspect of love, namely doubt. "Harat al 'Ushshaq"
(Lover's Lane) is the enactment of a philosophical treatise on
doubt. It is, however, clothed in the robes of a love story, such
as we read and see in every day life. The characters are a
middle-class government clerk, his very attractive wife, and a
series of other local stereotypes ranging from *shaykh al-harra*
(the neighborhood mayor) to the school teacher passing by the
baker's. The story is divided into seven parts, each narrating an
episode that is usually a consequence of the part preceding. We
soon discover that there is an underlying pattern that repeats
itself and helps create the impact of the ending. Mahfouz's
extensive use of dialogue to move the story forward is
effectively used in this story, giving it Socratic overtones.

The story opens on a scene of conjugal felicity. Husband
and wife are congratulating themselves on the bliss they have
lived in for the past five years. They can still remember
distinctly their courting days before marriage, then the first
years of their happy union:

He sighed, then a glimmer appeared in his dreamy look and said: Those days, I was just a clerk in the archives... poor, hard working, a husband passionately in love, even children we had decided to relegate to later times, no time for thinking, no time to look, work, work, work,... no thoughts, no worries, a limitless faith in everything, in you, in myself, in God; endless confidence in you, in myself, in God; everything was constant, solidly built (102).

Such was the state of things at the beginning. The emphasis on this pervading sense of security, the comforting belief that all is well with the world—in short an ordered universe where everything is in its proper place, in its right perspective—hence no need for worry or doubt of any kind. However this state of affairs is soon found to be not so permanent. Soon enough the husband hints at certain things he had been noticing about people in their alley. They apparently are willing to continue to gossip about their fellow neighbors; no one seems to escape their gossip. He then tells his wife of his growing sense of indignation with the rumors he has been hearing, and this first part ends with a heated discussion between the two, upon which he pronounces his verdict of divorce.

The second scene recapitulates the first, in that the once happy husband is now alone, but very sad. The Imam, Shaykh Marwan, visits him and offers to comfort 'Abd Allah. Furthermore he intervenes in favor of the divorced wife, protesting her innocence. In a question and answer repartee, he succeeds at the end of the conversation in convincing the doubting husband of the integrity of the wife. Using such convincing arguments as the following, the Imam brings about the change:

I know not where to begin. Shall I tell you that the men of God have perceptions of the heart that by far supersede the proofs of logic? But I fear that your faith in the force you imagine is not so. Many like to believe that they have faith, then you see them fall apart in face of their first trial. The true believer, O 'Abd Allah, moves mountains, overcomes death, shakes life itself... (113).

Thus through similar religio-philosophical arguments, Shaykh Marwan brings peace once more to the tortured existence of 'Abd Allah who bursts out saying at the end of part two: "God bless you Shaykh Marwan, you have saved me from darkness, and opened the doors of happiness and guidance" (118).

It is significant to note that all seven parts, like scenes of a play, open on the same setting. The alternating scenes of the husband and wife reconciled occur in the same living room that had witnessed their initial happiness. The wife always makes her appearance in a house coat, combing her hair, indicative of the relaxed atmosphere reigning in the household. During their conversations we learn that the husband has begun to be very critical of the Imam and refuses to go to his sessions of the *Quran*.

> I do not deny that I was fascinated by him, but he proceeded to unveil his true self. I have resisted boredom for months, waited in vain for him to say something new, but there was nothing different. A man who does his duty without putting any soul in it calls out his merchandise like a potato vendor (120).

He explains when he discovered this change: "a short while ago, but it is not easy to change and deny what we are used to believing in (120).

With such hints strewn all over the narrative, one cannot help but note the philosophical processes here at play. On one level the story is simply that of a marriage in danger of collapsing and, on a deeper level, the writer is investigating fundamentals. He questions matters involving faith, appearance and reality, for once he had highly considered the Imam, named his son after him, and now he doubts his motives, actions, and accuses his wife outright of having some kind of illicit encounter with Shaykh Marwan on their stairway. The outraged wife denies his allegations and once more leaves, a divorced woman for the second time.

In the fourth part, 'Abd Allah listens to the logic of 'Antar, the respected grade school teacher. He intercedes in favor of Shaykh Marwan, whom 'Abd Allah has shamelessly thrown out of his house. The school teacher is forced to make a revelation concerning the Imam that is intended to efface any doubts the husband may still have. 'Abd Allah is shocked to hear that the shaykh had been undergoing some treatment to cure him of a case of sexual impotence that had befallen him a year ago. In part five, Haniyya, the wife, is lovingly cajoling her new baby, named this time after the teacher 'Antar.

The ensuing part comes up with some disturbing revelations about the once trusted friends of 'Abd Allah. Shaykh al-Harra, shunned by all, accused of being an official informer to authorities, interrogates 'Abd Allah on the nature of his relationship with the teacher and the Imam. When asked what topics were usually discussed in their meetings, 'Abd Allah explains

> Indeed they are serious subjects, like liberty and the daily bread, good and evil; will immortality involve the soul only or both soul and body; do spirits exist in effect of merely symbolically (138).

Shayk al-Harra proceeds in his investigation, trying to corroborate some information he had collected concerning the two men, then just before leaving, announces that the two have been arrested.

This totally unexpected turn of events greatly disturbs 'Abd Allah and his wife. Once more 'Abd Allah's faith is shaken, once more he loses his bearings. He is left alone in this dilemma as the Shaykh al-Harra refuses to supply him with any incriminating evidence as to the alleged guilt of the once trusted friends. 'Abd Allah is once more in doubt and is left tormented by conflicting impulses.

The whole *harra* (alley) reacts in shock to the news; the inhabitants feel that they, too, have been cheated. Their heated arguments do not resolve the question, and they by no means reach a consensus as to whether the informer, Shaykh al-Harra, was solely to blame for his treachery, or whether the two culprits deserved their fate.

It is precisely that uncertainty that eats away at 'Abd Allah. The incident brings back a horde of suppressed doubts and emotions that had once troubled him. Sensing his mood, Haniyya turns to her husband pleadingly:

H: Here we are gradually returning to hell...
A: The important thing is that my life be built on a clear truth.
H: What's more important than all this is to appeal to wisdom during crises, and to always remember that you are a father.
A: Indeed, I am the father of Marwan, and 'Antar...
H: And it is a truth more important than anything else...
A: No, there exists a higher truth, which should not be undermined and I want to face it as it really is, even if it throws me in a circle fire.
H: I fear that our quest will lead us at the end to burning fire (149).

The corroding doubts that assail 'Abd Allah give him no peace. He is forever questioning and in search of truth. He is aware of the inherent contradictions of his life, he is "Antar's and Marwan's father," the namesakes of two highly respectable men, and yet today both stand accused. Maybe after all they both had affairs with his wife, and he was fooled all along?

Beneath all this commotion, Mahfouz is clearly saying much more than meets the eye. 'Abd Allah (his name means "Slave of God") is a man faced with the eternal quest for truth. Will he ever reach the bottom of this enigma? Will man be able to resolve the contradictions he finds inside and outside of himself?

As a final resort, 'Abd Allah turns to Shaykh al-Harra, seeking elucidation on the question of the arrest and its implications. The man who has the answer brings no relief. He is implacable n his stance in refusing to release any information that could be interpreted one way or another. He merely fulfills the function of supplying and collecting pertinent data that will eventually and hopefully lead to the truth. The author thus depicts Shaykh al-Harra as the teacher who knows all the answers but wants to see people reach them on their own, whereas 'Abd Allah wants immediate gratification:

A: Then how can one know the truth?
S: I know not what to say, but it is not enough to depend on others, you must exploit your personal talents and past experience...
A: The truth is I used to find ready answers from these men, answers that were decisive and comforting whenever I needed them (156).

Undaunted, 'Abd Allah persists in wanting to know whether the two men are completely guilty and hence the possible guilt of his wife. Insisting on not committing himself, Shaykh al-Harra informs him that chances are fifty-fifty that they are guilty, upon which 'Abd Allah finally resolves on a different course:

A: If my wife be guilty in the percentage of fifty percent she is at the same time innocent in the percentage of fifty percent.
S: And so?
A: And because I love her more than life itself, and because I cannot do without her unless I go mad, or commit suicide, I will therefore admit the possibility of innocence... (159).

And so ends 'Abd Allah's story. A compromise reached after long deliberations, trials and falterings. In the end, he says, he expects to be happy, but he estimates his happiness to be a fifty-percent possibility (199).

Mahfouz thus succeeds in subtly camouflaging his philosophical treatment of the question of Truth in the guise of a simple story involving the love of a man for a woman. One can speculate on the symbolic significance of the characters, and how the author infuses life and credibility in them. Haniyya (meaning happiness), the beautiful wife who is at the center of the conflict, is happiness itself. Without her 'Abd Allah finds life intolerable; madness and death are the only possible alternatives. Haniyya is inscrutable, evanescent; like happiness, she appears and disappears almost at will. Once he starts doubting her, life is never again the same. "Where ignorance is bliss, 'tis folly to be wise," Mahfouz seems to reiterate.

'Abd Allah seeks with all his might to recapture his old happiness, when he lived in an ordered universe, and neither questions nor doubts disturbed him. That was a time of innocence, before the fall. His lot, henceforth, is to live with knowledge that fills him with doubts; never again will he regain his "paradise lost."

Shaykh al-Harra, traditionally and proverbially the one who "knows absolutely everything about everybody," is appropriately chosen by Mahfouz as the informer. He informs not in the pejorative sense, although on the surface structure of the story he is considered such—an agent, a squealer. However on the deeper level, he leads 'Abd Allah to a way to some form of happiness. The all-knowing Shaykh al-Harra refuses to hand out "ready answers" to 'Abd Allah; he wants him, rather, to face the hard facts of life and find his own solutions. He is in effect telling him not to seek answers outside of himself; no one will provide him with comforting words that will prove true or reliable. 'Abd Allah is therefore forced to come to grips with the reality of his existential being.

ENDNOTES

CHAPTER 2: THE MOTHER OF THE BRIDE FRANTICALLY PREPARES

1 My thanks to Samer Shehata and Malak Hashem for their suggestions and insights.

2 The lyrics were collected while in Egypt during the summer of 1996. Some have appeared in an unpublished study by Muhammad Awad Khamis, "Psychology of the Contemporary Egyptian Woman" (1982). See also Sayed 'Oweiss, "Aspects of Egyptian Contemporary Society" *The National Sociological Magazine* (Cairo, 1975).

CHAPTER 4: I LIGHT TEN CANDLES

1 This article draws upon Hassan al-Shamy's *Folktales of Egypt* (Chicago 1980) and Khamis's "Psychology…" (see above).

2 *Extrait du Bulletin de l'Institut Français d'Archeologie Orientale* (Cairo 1953).

CHAPTER 5: A NEW VISION OF THE VEIL

1 The *khimar* is a veil that covers the head and falls over the shoulders.

2 The *burkaa* varies from Arab society to Arab society. In the early part of the 20th century in Egypt, for example, women wore a *burkaa* made of thin black net and positioned with a gold trinket on top of the nose. Bedouin women wore an embroidered cloth, sometimes covered with silver coins.

3 The *niqab* in its contemporary form is a total cover, with a mere slit for the eyes. We see some women from the Gulf countries wearing a form of the *niqab* today.

4 Abi Hurraira and Ibn Omar are the sources for this Hadith.

5 Here are the verses from the *Quran* that those who advocate the return of the *hijab* frequently site.

From the al-Nur sura, verse 31: "Direct the believing men to restrain their looks and to guard their senses. That is purer for them. Surely, Allah is well aware of that which they do. Direct the believing woman to restrain their looks and to guard their senses and not to disclose any part of their beauty or their adornments, save that which is apparent thereof. They should draw their headcoverings across their bosoms…"

From the al-Ahzab sura, verse 60: "O Prophet, direct thy wives and daughters and the women of the believers that they should pull down their outer cloaks from their heads over their faces. This will make is possible for them to be distinguished so that they will not be molested..."

References to the *Quran* from the Olive Branch Press edition translated by Muhammad Zafrulla Khan (1997).

CHAPTER 6: WOMEN IN THE DISCOURSE OF CRISIS

1 The Nahda, or the Arab literary renaissance, began in the Arab world in the mid-19th century, first in Lebanon and then Egpyt. The early pioneers experimented with modernizing the language, both prose and poetry. The impulse for change in all domains—literary, cultural, and political—aspired, among other things, to close the technological gap that existed beteen the Arab East and the European West.

2 Ismael Salem, *Naqd Mata'in Nasr Abu Zeid fi-l Qur'an wa-l Sunna wa-l Sahaba wa Aa'imat al-Muslimin* (Cairo: Dar al-Moukhtar al-Islami, 1993) 10–12.

3 This is further discussed in another chapter of the book.

4 See Farau Bin Ramadan, *Qadiyyat al-Mar'a fi Fikr al-Nahda* (Tunis: Dar Muhammad Aly al-Hamamy, 1998) 15.

5 See Abu-Zeid's article, "Nahda Project Bayn al-Tawfiq Wa-l Talfiq" in *al-Qahira* 119 (October 1992).

6 This categorization was first mentioned in the writings of Abi Hamid al-Ghazzali, especially in his compendium *Ihia' Ulum ad-Din*. See Abu-Zeid's *Mafhoum al-Nass: A Study in Quranic Sciences* (Beirut, Casablanca: Arab Cultural Center, 1990), especially Chapter 3.

7 Al-Tahir al-Haddad, *Al-Mar'aa fi al Shari'a wa al Mujtam'a* (al-Dar al-Tunisyia lil Nashr, 1992).

8 *Qiyas* at first meant analogical reasoning. Later it came to mean a syllogism, or syllogistic reasoning.

CHAPTER 7: NABIWIYYA MUSA AND AL-TAHIR AL-HADDAD IN A VIRTUAL DEBATE WITH ANWAR AL-GIUNDI

1 Kahmsun Shakhsiyya Misriyya, *Fifty Egyptian Personalities* (Cairo: Al-Qadi, 1989) 12.

CHAPTER 9: MODERN-DAY SHAHRAZADS

1 The shining peaks toward which men's ambitions aspire and get exhausted, the oasis that excites his thirst without ever quenching it.

The inexorable point—where, tragically faithful, one and the other meet—hope and disillusionment.

2 "A new thirst consumes the spirit."

CHAPTER 11: IMAGES OF WOMEN IN NORTH AFRICAN LITERATURE

1 Abdel Kabir Khatibi, *Le Roman Maghrébin* (Paris, Maspero, 1968).

2 See article by Zohra Riahi, Minutes of First Congress on Mediterranean Studies of Arabo-Berber Influence (Malto, 1972).

3 "I had to defend her, since she was equally a victim like the other women of the country where she came to reside..." Translated from Rachid Boudjedra, *La Répudiation* (Paris, Editions Denoel, 1969) 14.

4 "To look at others and to feel like an all-devouring stare." Translated from Assia Djebar, *Les Alouettes Naives* (Paris, Jullard, 1967) 65.

5 It is not scandalous to feel happy with oneself.

6 For I knew *apriori* that wars that end between nations are reborn within couples.

7 What will be the dance steps that will enable you to live and play at the same time?

8 See Mirelle Murray, ed., *A House of Good Proportion* (New York: Simon & Schuster, 1973).

CHAPTER 12: MASCULINE IDEOLOGY OR FEMININE MYSTIQUE?

1 My translations of the poems of Tuqan and Khamis appeared in *The Longman Anthology of World Literature*.

CHAPTER 13: WOMEN, LOVE, AND SEX IN YUSUF IDRIS'S CITY

1 *Afandi*: Turkish title commonly used to designate a man, dressed in Western clothes, rather than the *gallabiyya* of the peasant.

2 *Khatam Suliyman*, Solomon's ring, is a common analogy for the beauty of the mouth.

3 The tenant would conveniently send away Hamid for a pack of cigarettes, to have Fathiyya all to himself.

4 See Gaston Bachelard, *La terre et les rêveries du repos* (Paris: J. Corti, 1948) 121. Bachelard studies this universal theme of the return to the sources, and traces the relations between the meanings of the various aspects of this theme, including the return to one's mother: "*La réalité maternelle a été tout de suite multipliée par toutes les*

images d'intimité. La poesie de la maison réanime les intimitées et retrouve les grandes securitées d'une philosophie du repos."(Material reality was immediately multiplied by all intimate images. The poetry of the home reanimates those intimacies and rediscovers the great securities of a philosophy of repose.)

5 *Muqri*: a man who recites the verses of the *Quran* at funerals and other formal occasions.